Jeff VanVonderen
Dale & Juanita Ryan

SOUL REPAIR

Rebuilding Your Spiritual Life

IVP Books

An imprint of InterVarsity Press
Downers Grove, Illinois

InterVarsity Press
P.O. Box 1400, Downers Grove, IL 60515-1426
World Wide Web: www.ivpress.com
Email: email@ivpress.com

Design: Cindy Kiple
Images: Christopher Hudson/iStockphoto

ISBN 978-0-8308-3497-6

Printed in the United States of America ∞

Library of Congress Cataloging-in-Publication Data

Ryan, Dale, 1947-
  Soul repair: rebuilding your spiritual life / Dale Ryan, Juanita
Ryan, and Jeff VanVonderen.
    p. cm.
  Includes bibliographical references.
  ISBN 978-0-8308-3497-6 (cloth: alk. paper)
  1. Spiritual life—Christianity. I. Ryan, Juanita, 1949- II.
VanVonderen, Jeffrey. III. Title.
  248.8'6—dc22
              2008022652

P 25 24 23 22 21 20 19 18 17 16 15 14 13 12 11 10 9 8 7 6 5 4 3 2 1

Y 29 28 27 26 25 24 23 22 21 20 19 18 17 16 15 14 13 12 11 10 09 08

CONTENTS

ACKNOWLEDGMENTS

We want to express our gratitude to James Ryan, without whose assistance this book never would have been written. We are grateful also to Barbara Milligan and Cindy Bunch for helpful suggestions on early versions of the manuscript. Additional thanks to Robin and Nancy Wainwright, David Johnson, Peter Ryan, Dale Wolery, Cindy Evans, Genya Simonian and Mary Rae. We would be remiss not to acknowledge the enormous debt we owe to hundreds of people who have shared their stories with us in our roles as pastors, therapists and educators. To each of you we want to express our gratitude for your courage, your honesty and your trust; you have taught us a lot. It is our hope that through this book some of what you have taught us will benefit others. Finally, we want to thank the friends, counselors and spiritual partners who have offered us care and help through the years. Your love and support have been a vital part of our experience of grace.

INTRODUCTION

There is a time for everything,
and a season for every activity under heaven: . . .
a time to tear down and a time to build.

ECCLESIASTES 3:1, 3

W e seem to be hard-wired for the spiritual life—for having a relationship with God. It's down deep in us, at the heart of things.

It would be nice, therefore, if our relationship with God were simple. Some people, in fact, do experience spirituality in this way—as a stable source of encouragement, empowerment and nourishment. But that is not always the case. While it is true that spirituality can be a source of great blessing, it is also true that our spiritual lives can be the source of enormous suffering.

If your relationship with God—your spiritual life—has been uneasy, complex, confusing or hurtful, then this book was written for you. It is not, however, just about you; it is most definitely about us, the authors, as well. Although what we write about in this book is informed by our work as educators, pastors and counselors, it also reflects our personal experience. There is nothing theoretical or abstract for us in the things we talk about here. We each know from personal experience that spirituality can go bad. We've seen for ourselves how unhealthy spirituality can erode the foundations of our lives.

Thankfully, we are also coming to know what it is like for our spirituality to be a precious, grace-filled and practical resource in life. We have experienced God's Spirit infusing our spirits with gifts of humility, kindness and joy. We know the peace that comes when our spirits are freed from fears, shame and resentments. And we have tasted of the contentment and serenity that comes from sinking our roots deep in the soil of God's grace and love.

Experiencing God's grace and love, however, does not mean that we are no longer vulnerable to destructive spirituality. On the contrary, we are still in the process of fully understanding the ways that our spiritual brokenness affects our lives and the lives of others. We have found, however, that God is eager to bless us even in our spiritual brokenness. And that is perhaps the central theme of this book: even in our moments of deepest spiritual brokenness, when we can see nothing but ruin, God sees opportunities for blessing. Jesus put it simply:

> Blessed are the poor in spirit,
>> for theirs is the kingdom of heaven. (Matthew 5:3)

That statement does not match the instincts and expectations nurtured in us by our toxic spirituality, but it appears to be true. Our spiritual poverty is, in the eyes of God, an opportunity for blessing and not an occasion for judgment, shame or rejection. May God be praised.

A REALISTIC LOOK AT THE PROCESS

Because this book comes out of our personal experiences, you will find few simple answers to simple questions here. We understand how complex this topic is, and how difficult and painful it is to recognize that something has gone very wrong in our spiritual lives. And we understand how difficult it is to find the right kind of help when things go wrong—help that truly helps and doesn't make matters worse.

We know also how terrifying it can be when we begin to see that our spiritual lives may need to be torn down and rebuilt on healthier foundations. We understand the desperate desire to solve the problem by adding a fresh coat of paint or doing a minor remodel. Maybe even adding a room. But please, God, let it be something less drastic than tearing down and rebuilding. Unfortunately, if the problem is with our spiritual foundations, then anything less than demolition and rebuilding would probably be a waste of time—like the proverbial rearranging of deck chairs on the Titanic. Tearing down and rebuilding is what this book is about. In our spiritual lives there is a time to tear down. And there is a time to build.

One of Jesus' stories about the spiritual life is about a foolish man who built his house on the sand, and a wise man who built his house on a rock. When the winds and rain came, the man who built his house on sand was left homeless while the house built on rock withstood the harsh weather (Matthew 7:24-27). When he told this parable, Jesus was not talking to people who had rejected faith but to people who were attentive to their spiritual lives. It is not a story about people who refuse to build houses but about the kinds of foundations that make for stable houses. Like the religious people of Jesus' day, many of us who are active in our faith have built our houses on sand. In this book we explore what it means to build on the unstable sand of self-reliance and religious striving, and what it means to build on the solid rock of God's love and grace. We examine what spirituality looks like when it starts to collapse because of a faulty foundation, and we suggest some tools that might help us demolish unstable foundations and rebuild our spiritual lives on the foundation of God's grace.

No one sets out to build a spiritual house on sand. No one thinks, *Gee, I wish I could have a spiritual life that will fall apart when I need it the most.* Those of us who have built on an unstable foundation have done so unintentionally. We probably began our spiritual lives with the most solid piece of ground we could find, and we started building, hoping for the best. Some of us were tempted by a nice view or what seemed like a prime location. Some of us built our spiritual lives on land we inherited from our parents. Most of us probably built our spiritual homes in whatever was the most convenient spot, without first thoroughly examining the soil. There are lots of places to lay a spiritual foundation, but we have come to believe that the only stable foundation for the spiritual life is grace. Thankfully, grace has already been provided for us. We cannot earn it or compete for it or strive to deserve it, because grace is a gift freely given to us by God. This gift is a manifestation of God's rock-solid, faithful, unshakable, unconditional love for us. It is the rock on which we can build a stable spiritual life.

Rather than building our spiritual lives on the stable rock of God's love and grace, many of us find that we have built on the unstable soil of fear and shame. Fear and shame, which come in many forms, keep us from being able to trust God's love for us. We may fear that God is angry with us, is not *for* us, is not with us, is not truly loving toward us. Shame is, at its root, fear that we are not good enough, and never will be good enough, to have a meaningful relationship with God. These fears about ourselves are really forms of shame. We may fear that we are unlovable or that we have no value. We may experience ourselves as hopelessly damaged, without any possibility of repair.

The toxic combination of fear and shame lead to a variety of desperate efforts to stabilize our shaky spiritual house. We may try to get it right. We may try to control ourselves and others. We may try to please God and to earn God's love. We do these things because we really do want to have a viable spiritual life; we long to have a relationship with God that works. Unfortunately, most of these attempts to fix ourselves and to somehow earn God's love lead to a spiritual life that is destructive. After a while we find ourselves exhausted and discouraged, and we may feel even more alienated from God—in spite of our longing for our relationship with God to be one of the most stable and helpful in our lives.

What You'll Find in This Book

When our self-reliance and religious striving are driven by fear and shame, our lives show predictable patterns of spiritual dysfunction. In this book we begin our discussion of the spiritual rebuilding process by describing how it looks and feels when our spiritual lives are built on the unstable foundations of fear and shame. We look at four common types of destructive spirituality: spiritual abuse, spiritual anorexia, spiritual addiction and spiritual codependency.

There are many other types of destructive spirituality, but we have chosen to focus on these four because they are common enough that many people can identify one or more of these tendencies in their lives. If at first you don't clearly identify with any of these four patterns, keep in mind that each type exists on a continuum of severity. Most of us have probably experienced one or more of these forms of destructive spirituality to some degree, but often we are caught up in destructive spirituality without knowing it. We may only be aware of distressing symptoms such as anger, resentment, doubt, frustration, discouragement, exhaustion or despair. Any of these symptoms could indicate that the foundations of our spiritual lives are insecure and at risk.

After looking at these common forms of spiritual dysfunction, we need to thoroughly assess the foundations on which our spiritual lives are built. To what extent are our spiritual foundations rooted in God's love and grace? In what ways have these foundations become eroded or distorted? Following that assessment, we look at a blueprint for the rebuilding process. This blueprint may require some demolition of the existing foundations, and it may outline a project that, like any reconstruction project, requires a considerable amount of time and may be inconvenient and challenging. But the blueprint also promises that the security, stability and peace we experience in our relationship with God will grow stronger as the project continues.

After assessing the health of our existing spiritual foundations and examining a blueprint for the rebuilding process, we will see that few of us have good instincts when we first observe the structural flaws in our spiritual lives. So before we can actually begin to rebuild our spiritual lives, we will need to look at some things we are commonly tempted to do to fix our damaged spiritual lives—things that just don't work in the rebuilding process.

Finally, we look at spiritual tools that can help us rebuild our lives on the foundation of God's love and grace. These are some of the core tools of the Christian faith—tools with a long history in our tradition. Over the last two thousand years, these tools have helped millions of people come closer to God. Unfortunately, they have also been widely misused and have caused much spiritual harm, so we examine these tools carefully in order to understand how each has been misused and how it might be used appropriately to help us grow in our capacity to receive God's grace.

We are writing generally from the perspective of evangelical Protestantism; that is our spiritual heritage. However, we have tried not to assume that all our readers share this heritage. Though it may require some work on your part to reframe some things to fit better within your own theological tradition, we hope that this book will be helpful to everyone seeking to build a healthy spiritual life.

There is nothing magical about this book or about the rebuilding process we describe here. We don't have a simple "three keys to personal spiritual power" type of solution to offer. For those who have spent many years building a spiritual house on a faulty foundation, it will take some time to rebuild, and the rebuilding process we recommend is not an easy one. However, it is a process that is deeply rewarding, full of grace and rich with surprises. God will work in strange and wondrous ways in us as we rebuild, sometimes offering us support where we least expect to receive it. While rebuilding can be rough going, we are convinced that God is not a dispassionate observer of this kind of building project but rather an enthusiastic, passionate and loving participant.

One final point: This book is not a guide to getting our spiritual houses clean and orderly so that we can then approach God. It is not about becoming holy enough to convince God that spending time with us would be a good idea. This book is about making contact with a God who is willing to address the insecurity and decay of our spiritual lives and help us build something new. God does not wait until our spiritual houses are clean and orderly before making available to us all the love and grace we need. The biblical text is clear about this: God comes to us as we are. And God still comes to us—while our spiritual lives are disordered and dysfunctional—to fill us with as much grace as we are capable of receiving, and to encourage the process of growing in our capacity to receive even more grace in the future. Learning to receive that grace in practical ways is the main part of the work of rebuilding our spiritual lives. Our prayers are with you as you seek to rebuild your spiritual life on the stable and grace-filled foundation of God's love.

QUESTIONS FOR PERSONAL REFLECTION

1. How would you describe healthy spirituality?

2. How would you describe unhealthy or destructive spirituality?

3. What responses do you have to the metaphor of tearing down a spiritual life built on sand?

4. What thoughts and feelings do you have in response to the metaphor of rebuilding your spiritual life on grace?

PART 1

DISTORTED
SPIRITUALITY

1

ABUSIVE SPIRITUALITY

> *Jesus replied, "And you experts in the law, woe to you, because you*
> *load people down with burdens they can hardly carry, and you*
> *yourselves will not lift one finger to help them."*

LUKE 11:46

Bethany had been a dynamic lay leader among the women in her church for many years. She taught the only women's Bible study at the church and was almost always the featured speaker at the annual women's retreat.

Once in a while, one of the women would suggest that someone else might take a turn leading the Bible study or speaking at the retreat, but Bethany would respond by reminding them that God had called her to this ministry and that they should not second-guess God's decisions. In the Bible study, Bethany was impatient with women who had personal struggles, seeing it as a sign of a lack of faith. When women occasionally expressed concern about their troubled children, Bethany quoted Bible verses and explained that children don't misbehave if they have been instilled with biblical principles at a young age. According to Bethany, it was their own fault that their children were in trouble, and it was time that they took firm control of their children. It was also Bethany's habit to answer most questions that were raised during Bible study. There was no mystery about the Word of God; it said what it said, and Bethany was convinced that she knew exactly what it meant.

Over the years numerous women who had been active in women's ministry left the church. Several sent letters to the pastor, complaining that Bethany was domineering and judgmental, and that she made no room for others in leadership. The letters said that Bethany communicated that people needed to be perfect to go to her church. The pastor dismissed these letters as "sour grapes" or jealousy.

Then one day it became public knowledge that Bethany's daughter had been arrested for possession of methamphetamine. The church leadership responded to Bethany in the way she had been responding to the women at church for years: they told her that because she couldn't keep her own house in order, she didn't belong in leadership. Bethany was asked to resign from all her leadership positions. Bethany was devastated and soon left the church, unable to bear the shame she experienced.

When most of us think about spirituality going bad, we think first about people using spiritual authority to harm others. It is all too common that people in positions of spiritual authority use their positions to disempower and manipulate others, rather than to support them and build them up. Battered wives are told by their pastors that Jesus wants them to be more submissive; children abused by a parent are told that God expects them to obey their parents; whole congregations fear for their souls if they so much as utter a sigh of discontentment about their leaders—all of these situations are sadly familiar in the Christian community.

We know that there are extreme forms of abusive spirituality— religious cults that end in mass suicide, and religious organizations that exist to meet the financial, sexual or ego needs of their leaders.

But there are also more subtle forms of spiritual abuse, like the kind practiced by Bethany. These abuses generally go unnoticed and unexamined. They are, for many people, "just the way things are."

Jeff's experience of growing up in an abusive church suggests what it feels like to take in the basic message of spiritual abuse:

> My family lived in a town of six hundred people, and we drove two miles every Sunday to a town of two hundred people where they had seven churches. The marquee in the front of our church said "Independent, fundamental, Bible-believing, soul-winning, sin-hating, separated Baptist church." In this town of two hundred people there was another Baptist church—directly across the street—and their sign said the same thing: "Independent, fundamental, Bible-believing, soul-wining, sin-hating, separated Baptist church." But we had nothing to do with those across-the-street people. I went to school for twelve years with kids from that church across the street and never made friends with any of them. I never went across the street and into that building, because we were more separated, more fundamental, and more sin-hating than they were. Everybody but us was outside the kingdom. We were it.
>
> Our pastor would point at you from the pulpit if you were chewing gum, and tell you that you were going to hell. It was scary until the age of eleven or twelve, when I decided to let that stuff roll off my back. When he pointed me out, I would think, *Yeah, right. He's stupid.* But one of the remnants of all that judgment was that I was being trained to be judgmental.
>
> Being trained to be judgmental is one of the most damaging parts of spiritual abuse. It hurts like crazy to be judged, but it hurts just as much or more to be judgmental. In order to be

judgmental, you have to work hard to maintain an image that allows you the luxury of feeling somehow superior. All those crazy thoughts you have, no one can ever know about those. All the anger and frustration and struggles you have, no one can ever see any of that. When you've been taught to be judgmental, you have to keep it all bottled up inside you so that you are always outwardly in a position to make others look "less than."

But what got to me, more than the things that were said from the pulpit, was having my relationship with Christ taken hostage. After I made some bad choices as a teenager, Christ was constantly used as a threat to get me to behave. It was as if my salvation were on loan. It was called into question all the time. Even though we were taught that there was nothing we could do to earn grace, in practice the opposite was true. Everything we did was weighed and measured to see if we deserved to keep grace.

All spiritual abuse has its roots in the same soil. Whenever we give others the message that their relationship with God depends on something other than God's love and grace—or that God's love and grace need to be earned in some way—we are perpetrating spiritual abuse. This message can be communicated from the pulpit or at the dinner table, with fists or with whispers. Whether or not there is accompanying sexual, emotional or physical abuse, the message of spiritual abuse is always the same: "God won't love you, unless . . ." or "God will only love you if . . ."

Spiritual abuse is usually a systemic problem. Rarely do we find that only one member of a church or family is spiritually abusive. Commonly, as the message of a few is heard and accepted by others, the entire system comes to believe and act as if God were really an unloving, absent or abusive God. Once the message is accepted, it is repeated

in a variety of forms—some subtle and some not—by those who have
accepted it. In this way, spiritual abuse is handed down the chain of
authority, from pulpit to pew and from one generation to the next.

People who are caught up in abusive spirituality—both the abusers
and the abused—are often judgmental because they fear that God is
harsh and punitive, and they fear that they are defective. They are not
able to trust God's mercy and therefore cannot experience, practice
or give mercy.

In Luke's story about Simon the Pharisee (Luke 7:36-50), we see
clearly the experience of the abuser and the abused. Simon is a religious leader and teacher who has a great deal of power in his community. When a woman who is known to be a sinner comes in and
weeps at Jesus' feet, Simon judges her. He does not see the woman
as a fellow human being in need of grace, but as a sinner who doesn't
warrant grace.

> Now one of the Pharisees invited Jesus to have dinner with him,
> so he went to the Pharisee's house and reclined at the table. When
> a woman who had lived a sinful life in that town learned that Je-
> sus was eating at the Pharisee's house, she brought an alabaster
> jar of perfume, and as she stood behind him at his feet weeping,
> she began to wet his feet with her tears. Then she wiped them
> with her hair, kissed them and poured perfume on them.
>
> When the Pharisee who had invited him saw this, he said to
> himself, "If this man were a prophet, he would know who is touch-
> ing him and what kind of woman she is—that she is a sinner."
>
> Jesus answered him, "Simon, I have something to tell you."
>
> "Tell me, teacher," he said.
>
> "Two men owed money to a certain moneylender. One owed
> him five hundred denarii, and the other fifty. Neither of them

had the money to pay him back, so he canceled the debts of both. Now which of them will love him more?"

Simon replied, "I suppose the one who had the bigger debt canceled."

"You have judged correctly," Jesus said.

Then he turned toward the woman and said to Simon, "Do you see this woman? I came into your house. You did not give me any water for my feet, but she wet my feet with her tears and wiped them with her hair. You did not give me a kiss, but this woman, from the time I entered, has not stopped kissing my feet. You did not put oil on my head, but she has poured perfume on my feet. Therefore, I tell you, her many sins have been forgiven—for she loved much. But he who has been forgiven little loves little."

Then Jesus said to her, "Your sins are forgiven."

The other guests began to say among themselves, "Who is this who even forgives sins?"

Jesus said to the woman, "Your faith has saved you; go in peace." (Luke 7:36-50)

Simon sees everything through the grid of judgment. He thinks of others in terms of right and wrong, good and bad, superiority and inferiority. Simon believes himself to be right, good and superior, and others (probably including Jesus!) to be wrong, bad and inferior. Simon does not know he is just as broken and in need of grace as the woman who is weeping at Jesus' feet. He reacts defensively to this truth because his fears and shame make his spiritual brokenness too painful to face. His defense is to be scrupulous, arrogant, prideful, self-righteous and judgmental. This kind of defense against brokenness leads directly to the abuse of others—through superior attitudes, harsh words, exclusion and devaluing. When this kind of judgmentalism is encouraged in the name of God, God becomes a kind of blunt instrument that can be used to hurt, punish, shame and control others.

One of Juanita's experiences illustrates how judgmentalism, even in subtle forms, can plant the seeds of spiritual abuse:

> I remember driving alone one morning, my mind drifting between thoughts, when I suddenly had a strong sense that God was saying to me, "You are judging that person you were just thinking about." As I thought back to what had been going through my mind, I realized that I had been thinking of someone I knew—someone who looked to me for spiritual help—as if I were in some way superior and as if he were inferior. I had been judging myself as "better than" and this person as "less than," and I realized how easy this type of judgment was for me. This was certainly not the first time I had judged someone! I acknowledged my sin and thanked God for bringing it to my attention. This particular judgment was private—it existed only in my mind—but judgments like this are the seeds of spiritual abuse.
>
> While reflecting on this event, it occurred to me that in the Gospel story about the woman weeping at Jesus' feet, Simon does not speak an abusive word. But he is filled with judgment. And judgment always finds a way to be expressed. The woman who came to weep at Jesus' feet would find herself disempowered and devalued by this person who had religious power over her and over others, just as the person I was judging would have been in danger of feeling disempowered and devalued by me.

The experience of being judged and devalued is the experience of being shamed. To feel shame is to feel exposed and to be seen as "less than." Shame is difficult to adequately define, but one good attempt comes from Gershen Kaufman, in his book *Shame: The Power of Caring*, who says that shame is rooted in "sudden unexpected exposure" that leaves us feeling "painfully diminished in our own eyes and in the eyes of others as well." He continues, "To live with shame is to feel alienated and defeated, never quite good enough to belong. And secretly we feel to blame. The deficiency lies within ourselves alone. Shame is without parallel a sickness of the soul."

This emphasis on shame as a "sickness of the soul" is helpful for our purposes. Shame leads to many kinds of spiritual dysfunction, including the kind of judgmentalism we see in spiritual abuse.

Even though Simon is secretly shaming both the woman and Jesus, Jesus does not respond to Simon's judgment by shaming him. Instead, Jesus responds with mercy and goes to the heart of the problem. "Simon," Jesus says, "do you see this woman?" Jesus invites Simon to expand his spiritual vision so that he can see this person of infinite value, who is loved and cherished by God and is capable of great love. This is how Jesus sees the woman: he sees, receives and responds to her love. Jesus invites us to see each other in the same way—through the eyes of God's love and mercy. Whenever we see each other as less than God's beloved children, we run the risk of doing spiritual harm.

A BIBLICAL OVERVIEW OF SPIRITUAL ABUSE

The Bible is full of examples of spiritual abuse. There are stories of spiritual leaders who exploited people for their own gain; there are stories about authority being misused in order to get things done in the name of God that weren't really part of God's agenda at all; and there are stories about people who trivialize the pain of others. Jeremiah, for example, talked about those who heal other people's wounds superficially:

> They dress the wound of my people
>> as though it were not serious.
> "Peace, peace," they say,
>> when there is no peace. (Jeremiah 6:14)

This kind of failure by spiritual leaders to take seriously the pain of others is spiritual neglect, a form of spiritual abuse. God's complaint about many of the leaders of Israel was that they were not using the authority they had been given for the benefit of the weak, for those who lacked a voice; the leaders were instead using their authority for their own purposes. The result at that time was the same as it is now: spiritual exhaustion rooted in misconceptions about who God is and what God wants from us.

In the New Testament, Jesus reserves his strongest language for criticism of religious leaders whose spirituality is abusive. For example, in Matthew 23:27 Jesus describes the Pharisees as "whitewashed tombs." This expression might seem like merely a picture of hypocrisy—being different on the outside than on the inside—but there is more to it than this. People at that time believed that if you touched a tomb you would be defiled. So Jesus is not only calling the Pharisees hypocrites; he is saying that if you fall under their influence, you could become spiritually harmed.

"Ferocious wolves" is another expression Jesus used for spiritually abusive leaders (Matthew 7:15). Expressions like these helped Jesus draw a stark contrast between the abusive and appropriate uses of authority. Jesus clearly taught that spiritual authority is not designed to burden people spiritually or to discourage them or to use them for personal gain. Rather, the purpose of spiritual authority is to build people up, to encourage them and to set them free.

Spiritual abuse was a central concern for the early church. The apostle Paul's primary adversaries thought he put too much emphasis on grace. They tried to correct his teaching, explaining that the good news is not simply about what God has done but also what we need to do. In some texts Paul's opponents were called the "circumcision party," because they believed it was necessary to perform the religious ritual of circumcision to secure God's approval. Today, circumcision is no longer thought of as the Cadillac of spiritual disciplines, but many religious communities invent other kinds of religious requirements or behavioral demands. The formal theology or "statement of faith" of many spiritually abusive communities may affirm the centrality of grace in Christian spirituality, but in practice they communicate that God's love is somehow contingent on our performance. The members of the early Christian community faced the same dynamic when they dealt with the circumcision party.

TYPES OF SPIRITUAL ABUSE

Abuse can be appropriately called spiritual abuse when it takes one of two forms. First, abuse of any kind in an explicitly spiritual context can be spiritual abuse. The spiritual context could be a church, a religious retreat or a religious institution. Or the spiritual context could be created by the presence of a person in a position of spiritual authority, like a pastor or a Sunday school teacher or even a parent, who perpetrates abuse, regardless of where the abuse happens. When any kind of abuse—emotional, sexual or physical—happens within the context of a faith community, it is a form of spiritual abuse. Either the spiritual location or the spiritual role of the abuser can communicate that the abusive treatment is somehow approved of or permitted by God, and this communicates the basic, abusive message: that God is not a God of love and grace.

Second, any kind of abuse that does damage to someone's relationship with God is spiritual abuse—even if the abuse happens outside a spiritual context. This is an especially important point in the case of the spiritual abuse of children. Because children are actively engaged in the important process of forming a sense of who God is, any form of child abuse does damage to their developing spirituality and is for that reason a form of spiritual abuse. Parents who threaten their children by picturing God as a kind of bogeyman who will punish them if they misbehave can do damage to their children's emerging spirituality. Children can easily pick up the message that God is graceless, that love is conditional, that performance is the most important thing or that perfection is what is expected. All of these messages can get in the way of spiritual growth and development founded on the grace of God.

Spiritual abuse communicates the message that God does not love and accept us as we are, that we must work to earn God's approval and that God's love and grace are not enough. Once the devaluing messages of spiritual abuse become internalized, we start to live as if the messages were true, and this inevitably leads us to pass abusive messages on to others. Eventually, it becomes difficult for us to live outside a spiritually abusive environment or to even consider the possibility that God might actually love us just as we are.

A pastor friend of ours began his recovery journey while serving at a small church, and his experiences provide a useful example of how spiritual abuse can become deeply embedded in a person's spiritual life. As a result of the personal changes this pastor made, and his growing awareness of God's grace, his sermons became more and more filled with a sense of God's grace. One Sunday, a long-standing member of the congregation approached this pastor after the morning service and informed him that she would be leaving the church.

"Okay," the pastor replied. "I want you to know that I respect your decision. However, if you'd like to share your reasons for leaving, it might be helpful to me."

The woman's face hardened. "Fine," she said. "I used to be able to come to this church knowing that I would leave feeling bad about myself. You reminded me of how sinful I was, and how I needed to try hard to be better. It helped me to keep a lid on things throughout the week. But you just don't preach that way anymore, and it's making me anxious. I don't think I'm getting what I need to be a good Christian anymore."

The woman also communicated her suspicion that this pastor was not preaching from the Bible like he had in the past. She was convinced that if he were really preaching from the Bible, she would have bad feelings about herself—the shame—that she needed on Sunday mornings. She knew what the Bible was about. It was about guilt and shame, and this is what she thought she needed in order to function spiritually.

This story shows how, after years in an abusive system, the abusive messages become internalized and form a template for what is considered normal. To this woman, grace was suspect, dangerous, and she experienced guilt and shame as normative and godly; a loving God would be too much to ask for. Instead, she sought a new shaming environment that matched her internal template, which robbed her of a healthy spiritual life.

HOW SPIRITUAL ABUSE HAPPENS

For some of us, our faith journey began with an understanding that we didn't need to do anything to earn God's love and grace. This good news came to us as a blessing. We knew we needed grace, and God provided it for us. At that point our hearts were tender toward God, and we wanted to do the things that God desired of us. Even if we weren't capable of making all the changes we needed to make on our own power, we suddenly found ourselves wanting to do the right thing.

Unfortunately, that desire made us susceptible to people who said, "Hey, you want to know God's agenda? Well, we know more about that than anybody else. We'll tell you what God wants, and encourage you to work really hard to make it happen." Then—very subtly and with good intentions—we began the game of trying to measure up.

The belief that we must work for God's approval immediately creates two problems. First, as soon as we begin to work for God's approval, we begin to judge others. We work hard to get grace, and so we feel justified in condemning anyone not working as hard as we are working. Second, working to earn God's grace usually means that we have to hide many unpleasant things about ourselves in order to measure up to expectations. Hiding or suppressing our sins rather than confessing them leads to a dual life. We become convinced that if anyone ever knew the truth about what goes on inside us, they would condemn us. Out of fear, we become defensive, and whenever anyone points out a problem with our behavior, however lovingly, we lash out and demonize them. Instead of admitting that we have a problem, we make them the problem. In this way we become perpetrators of spiritual abuse.

HOW DO I KNOW IF I'M SPIRITUALLY ABUSIVE?

We become spiritually abusive when we lose track of the fact that God loves us no matter what. For example, if Pastor Fred forgets that he can't earn grace and begins to believe that God measures him by the size of his congregation, he may become abusive in order to get those numbers. To make his congregation grow, Fred must motivate his people to bring in new members. Because he believes that God's approval rests on the size of his congregation, Fred transfers this graceless belief to his people. In his sermons he finds ways to suggest that the value and acceptance of true Christians in God's eyes are related to how many people they bring to church with them. If the congregation really cares about others, and if they really believe in the Word of God, they will invite more people to come with them on Sunday morning.

As simply as that, Fred has chosen to disempower his congregation. He is no longer there to meet the needs of the congregation; he is using the congregation to meet his own needs. Pastor Fred is trying to control the members of his congregation and the size of his congregation in order to feel okay about his relationship with God. In the process he is manipulating other people's spiritual lives rather than resting in the love and grace of God.

Spiritual abusers usually are not conscious of what they are doing. Few who accept leadership positions in a Christian community are thinking, *I'm looking forward to manipulating people so that they get their value from how I tell them to behave rather than from Christ.* Most spiritual abusers have good intentions. They see their actions as an expression of concern for the well-being of others. Few would be able to recognize, let alone articulate, that they are putting their faith in something they are doing rather than in God, and that they are encouraging others to do the same.

Anytime we are in a position of spiritual leadership or influence and we move away from grace, we are in danger of becoming abusive. We need to regularly ask ourselves several questions:

- Do I need to rely on anything other than God's love to be okay in my relationship with God?

- Would it feel catastrophic if I made a mistake?

- Am I unwilling to give up control over other people's behavior?

- Do I feel compelled to pretend that I don't struggle or have problems?

- Am I judgmental toward others, negatively assessing their spiritual standing compared to my own?

- Do I have a need to "get it absolutely right" in my relationship with God?

If we answer yes to any of these questions, we may be suffering from the destructive dynamic of abusive spirituality.

HOPE FOR ABUSERS AND THE ABUSED

Whether we are perpetrators or survivors (or both), recognizing that spiritual abuse is part of our life story is a painful one. We have been harmed by the people we trusted the most, and we have taken that hurt and passed it on to the people who trusted us. If we are caught in this abusive cycle, our relationship with God is probably distorted by shame, rejection and judgmentalism. Healing from this kind of harm can be difficult and time-consuming. But healing is possible. In later chapters, we will discuss the healing process in more detail. At this time, we can best describe how people heal from spiritual abuse by returning to Bethany's story. Bethany had left the church where she had been spiritually abusing other women. Her daughter's addiction to methamphetamine led the church to believe that Bethany was unfit to serve in a leadership capacity. As you might imagine, Bethany was depressed after the church abandoned her. She couldn't sleep at night and had trouble getting out of bed in the morning. She had no appetite and stayed at home all day.

A woman who had been driven away from the church by Bethany almost five years earlier heard about Bethany's daughter and the church's response, and decided to reach out to Bethany. She called

Bethany and told her that her own son was a drug addict. This woman had been attending a church support group for parents of drug addicts, and when she invited Bethany to go with her to a meeting, Bethany accepted.

At the support group Bethany met many other mothers and some fathers who had suffered the pain of loving an addicted child and who were surviving by depending on a loving God. Bethany heard at the meeting that it was possible to depend on God for practical help, that God desires to give us gifts like wisdom and guidance, compassion and serenity. She also heard people talking about their struggle to trust God's active love because they had served other kinds of gods for a long time. Some people in the group even said they had to let go of all their preconceived ideas about God and to open themselves up to new experiences of God. This bothered Bethany greatly. She felt that she had the correct beliefs about God and didn't need any group to tell her something that might lead her astray. But Bethany was also in a lot of pain. She heard the other parents talking about their experience of God's love and grace, and she wanted to have an experience like that. For all her convictions about who God is, Bethany had no experience to compare to theirs.

Through weekly attendance at this group, Bethany began to realize that she had been serving a god who was harsh, condescending and abandoning. She also saw that she had behaved exactly like the god she served. She had judged, corrected and condemned. Because of her daughter's drug addiction, Bethany now knew how it felt to receive that kind of treatment. Bethany was remorseful and angry. She didn't want to serve an abusive god anymore.

The support group for parents of addicts had a set of tools they used for growing spiritually. They all came to realize that they were power-less over their children's addictions and that they needed to surrender their own lives and their children's lives to God's loving care. Bethany began a daily practice of asking God to help her rest in the fact that God was loving and trustworthy, and then releasing her daughter into God's hands. The group also practiced regular confession and placed a strong emphasis on making amends for harm done. Over time, as Bethany listened to the honesty and humility in the confessions of the other parents, her heart softened. Judgment gave way to compassion; condemnation was replaced by an awareness of the power and availability of grace. Slowly, as she listened to other people's confessions, Bethany began forming a mental list of people she had harmed, and she realized that her daughter belonged on that list. Bethany then asked a group member to help her consider the kind of approach that might be appropriate in making amends to each person.

When Bethany went out to make amends to her daughter, she was filled with fear. She had raised her daughter under the same judgment and criticism that she had placed on the women at church, and as a result Bethany's daughter had been unwilling to talk to her for the past several years. In her imagination Bethany played out every possible bad outcome of meeting with her daughter, and each new vision was a torture. Bethany racked her brain to think of some way she could make up for the harm she had caused her daughter, but nothing, including an apology, seemed sufficient; there was nothing she could do. She had hurt her daughter, and it was not in her power to make things right again. Bethany realized that all she could do was to show up and honestly, humbly acknowledge that she had hurt her daughter.

In order to get out of her car, Bethany had to remind herself that maybe there really was a God who could help her through this. Making amends seemed like a test to see if such a God existed. As she got out of her car, Bethany prayed for help and wished there was an easier way to experience God. Yet this was the first time Bethany had actually relied on the love and support of others, and the first time she had taken a step of faith, trusting that a loving God would help her and her daughter.

Bethany and her daughter met for lunch. They ate and talked, and for the first time in her daughter's life they had a conversation in which the focus was not on her daughter's problems. In this conversation the focus was on Bethany's abusive behavior toward her daughter. Bethany spoke as candidly as she was able. She said she knew that making amends meant more than just saying she was sorry. She said she had no idea what she could do to make up for the harm she had caused, but she was committed to finding a better way to be a mother to her daughter. Bethany told her daughter that she loved her and that her daughter's arrests and addiction hadn't changed that.

When lunch was over and Bethany and her daughter went their separate ways, Bethany was left with a strong sense of God's presence. She had asked for help, and God had provided the grace, humility and courage she needed for being honest. As she sat alone in her car, Bethany felt comforted by the God of love and grace that she had read about in Scripture but could never really comprehend until now.

Bethany continued to attend her support group long after her daughter stopped using drugs. She found that this group provided her with a place where she could be honest about herself and her experiences without fear of judgment. Bethany also discovered that the longer she practiced the spiritual tools she was learning in the group, the more she could be useful to the parents who were new to the group. By telling her own story and the story of her spiritual rebuilding process, Bethany was able to give hope and strength to many other parents who were struggling with their children's drug addiction. In time, Bethany also started a small group for people who had experienced spiritual abuse. She found that by sharing her story as a spiritual abuser and as a survivor of spiritual abuse, she was creating a safe place for others, people like herself, to rebuild their spiritual lives. Telling the truth and serving others is now a source of pleasure and fulfillment for Bethany. Her relationship with God is growing as she shares God's grace with the people in her life who need and want that grace.

QUESTIONS FOR PERSONAL REFLECTION

1. The woman who wept at Jesus feet (in Luke 7) and the women who were in Bethany's Bible study experienced spiritual abuse. In what ways, if any, do you relate to the experiences of these women?

2. Simon the Pharisee and Bethany were judgmental and spiritually abusive. In what ways, if any, do you relate to them?

3. What do you think were some of the most important changes Bethany made that allowed her to break out of the cycle of abuse?

4. Read the story of Jesus eating with Simon the Pharisee in Luke 7:36-50. As you read, try to imaginatively place yourself in the story as the woman who weeps at Jesus feet. Listen to what Jesus says to you and about you. Then reflect on this experience. What was it like for you?

5. Read the same text again, trying to imaginatively place yourself in the story as Simon. Listen to what Jesus says to you. Then reflect on this experience. What was it like for you?

2

ANOREXIC SPIRITUALITY

It is surrender to love that I really resist. I am willing to accept
measured doses of love as long as it doesn't upset the basic framework of
my world. That framework is built on the assumption that people get
what they deserve. That's what I really want. I want to earn
what I get.

DAVID G. BENNER

Ted was a middle-aged man and had lived what he called a "good
enough" life. He owned and ran his own business, he was on the board
of trustees at his church, and he occasionally led a men's Bible study.
When people spoke about Ted, they remarked that he was a nice guy
who would go out of his way to help someone. Ted was a kind and
generous person, but he felt dry and empty inside. His life seemed like
a dull routine to him. He went to work, he came home, he watched
TV, and he went to bed. Sometimes Ted lay awake at night, staring at
the ceiling and wondering why he didn't feel closer to God.

One Sunday, when the pain of his spiritual dryness was particularly
strong, Ted's pastor preached a sermon on receiving from God. Ted's
pastor said that it was not uncommon to have trouble receiving from
God, and that the church was about to start some spiritual direction
groups whose purpose was to help people receive spiritual nourish-

ment from God. The pastor said the groups would be structured so that people had the opportunity to share as openly as they chose and then to meditate on Scripture together.

Ted found himself growing increasingly angry throughout the sermon. Just talking about receiving from God felt dangerous to Ted. The pastor, according to Ted, was painting a picture of a soft, fuzzy, Santa Claus type of God who just loved giving stuff to people without asking them to do anything in return. Ted was sure this kind of thinking would lead to a congregation full of passive, needy people. *We shouldn't even be thinking about receiving from God,* he thought. *We need to stay focused on our responsibility to give to God.*

Ted suffers from spiritual anorexia.

Most people have heard something about anorexia in relation to food. However, anorexia, like addiction, is a process that can express itself in relation to many things other than food. Anorexia is a compulsive resistance to some form of nurture, a self-manufactured starvation. Someone who is anorexic in relation to food is resisting physical nurture. Someone who is spiritually anorexic is resisting spiritual nurture. An anorexic in relation to food can live in a world full of food and still starve to death. A spiritual anorexic lives in a world full of the love and grace of God but is starving spiritually. Like anorexia in relation to food, anorexic spirituality exists on a continuum of severity. A food anorexic may be able to eat enough to maintain a low weight, may knowingly or unknowingly resist the experience of being hungry, may feel terrible anxiety when even thinking about food or may be unable to eat at all. In the same way a spiritual anorexic may be able to take in some small doses of spiritual nurture, may knowingly or unknowingly resist the need for love and grace, or may be extremely anxious at the very thought of receiving from God.

Jesus provided a helpful illustration of one of the central dynamics

of spiritual anorexia when he told the parable of the waiting father
(Luke 15:11-32). Often when people read this parable, they focus only
on the first half of the story, in which the younger son leaves home and
spends his inheritance foolishly. But there are two sons in the story,
and the second half of the parable is about the son who stayed home.
The key to understanding this parable is to notice that both of the sons
have essentially the same strategy for how they are going to be part of
the father's family. The younger son's strategy is clear. As the prodigal
walks home, he practices a speech that reflects his fears about his father and his shame about himself—that he is a worthless failure who
is beyond being loved. He plans to say to his father, "I am unworthy to
be your son, so I will be your servant." A servant's job is to give. So the
younger son plans to give and give and give to his father, and thereby
acquire acceptance.

When the older son thinks about his experience in his father's family, he also sees himself as a servant. While the younger son was off
squandering his inheritance, the older son has been at home acting
like a servant. He has been giving and giving and giving to the father.
He has been using the same strategy that his younger brother hopes to
adopt in the future. Neither son seems to have considered the possibility that his father loves him and desires to be the one who gives. Both
sons seem profoundly resistant to receiving from their father.

> Jesus continued: "There was a man who had two sons. The
> younger one said to his father, 'Father, give me my share of the
> estate.' So he divided his property between them.
>
> "Not long after that, the younger son got together all he had,
> set off for a distant country and there squandered his wealth in
> wild living. After he had spent everything, there was a severe
> famine in that whole country, and he began to be in need. So

he went and hired himself out to a citizen of that country, who sent him to his fields to feed pigs. He longed to fill his stomach with the pods that the pigs were eating, but no one gave him anything.

"When he came to his senses, he said, 'How many of my father's hired men have food to spare, and here I am starving to death! I will set out and go back to my father and say to him: Father, I have sinned against heaven and against you. I am no longer worthy to be called your son; make me like one of your hired men.' So he got up and went to his father.

"But while he was still a long way off, his father saw him and was filled with compassion for him; he ran to his son, threw his arms around him and kissed him.

"The son said to him, 'Father, I have sinned against heaven and against you. I am no longer worthy to be called your son.'

"But the father said to his servants, 'Quick! Bring the best robe and put it on him. Put a ring on his finger and sandals on his feet. Bring the fattened calf and kill it. Let's have a feast and celebrate. For this son of mine was dead and is alive again; he was lost and is found.' So they began to celebrate.

"Meanwhile, the older son was in the field. When he came near the house, he heard music and dancing. So he called one of the servants and asked him what was going on. 'Your brother has come,' he replied, 'and your father has killed the fattened calf because he has him back safe and sound.'

"The older brother became angry and refused to go in. So his father went out and pleaded with him. But he answered his father, 'Look! All these years I've been slaving for you and never disobeyed your orders. Yet you never gave me even a young goat so I could celebrate with my friends. But when this son of yours who has squandered your property with prostitutes comes home, you kill the fattened calf for him!'

"'My son,' the father said, 'you are always with me, and everything I have is yours. But we had to celebrate and be glad, because this brother of yours was dead and is alive again; he was lost and is found.'" (Luke 15:11-32)

The father has essentially the same response to both his sons. In their fear and shame both sons anticipate that their father will be punitive and withholding. But the opposite is true. The father Jesus describes is loving and generous. This father delights to give good gifts to his children because he loves them dearly. He gives to the younger son a joyful embrace, a robe, a ring and a party. And to the older son he says, "Everything I have is yours." In other words: "I am the father. I delight in giving all I have to you. You are my child, not my servant. I want you to receive my love and my gifts." Jesus clearly told this story to teach us something about what life is like in God's family. God loves to give. We are God's precious children. As much as we might prefer to be the one who gives in our relationship with God, our job is to grow in our capacity to receive.

Receiving from God is a problem for many of us, and so we resist it; we resist spiritual nurture. We are much more comfortable performing for God than receiving from God, probably for many reasons. Performing for God can be done from a position of relative strength, but receiving can be perceived as a kind of weakness. Giving to God gives us something to feel good about, but receiving can leave us feeling like a burden. Performing for God allows us to feel in control and protects us from the vulnerability of our needs, but receiving may accentuate our neediness. For some people this resistance to receiving from God may mean only that they need to be reminded periodically to allow

God to nurture them. But for people who struggle with spiritual anorexia, this resistance to receiving from God is a much more serious problem. It can become spiritually life-threatening.

People who struggle with anorexia do not always look anorexic. People who are physically anorexic do not always look undernourished, and the same is true of people who are spiritually anorexic. In the 1990s an American television station aired a documentary about the war in Bosnia. The film included some scenes at an orphanage, where perhaps thirty-five or forty infants, all gathered in one room, lay tightly wrapped, as was the local custom, each in his or her own crib. The room was absolutely silent. At first it seemed amazing that there could be a room full of such satisfied infants in a war zone, in an understaffed, underfunded orphanage. The infants showed every sign of contentment. But things were not as they seemed. These infants had cried until they could cry no longer. No one was there to respond to their needs. There was no nourishment available, and so they eventually stopped crying. The silence was not a sign of contentment but of despair.

This image is a painful but useful metaphor for all kinds of anorexia. Spiritual anorexia is a kind of giving up on the possibility that God will meet our spiritual needs. We may look content, but just like those infants, we may not have any energy left to long for nurture, and so we give up. Those of us who struggle with spiritual anorexia conclude that no more spiritual nurture is available. We must make do with the little we have. As a result, we live with a kind of lethargy, a resignation, a passivity, a hopelessness and despair that can sometimes be mistaken for contentment. We show up week after week at the spiritual dinner table, but we never eat.

CHARACTERISTICS OF SPIRITUAL ANOREXIA

Like physical anorexia, spiritual anorexia usually involves a mixture of resistance to nurture, a distorted self-concept and a high need for control.

Resistance to spiritual nurture. Resistance to spiritual nurture can vary from person to person. For some people spiritual anorexia manifests itself as a kind of resignation. Having lived with spiritual deprivation for so long, they conclude that being passive and reducing their expectations is less painful than continuing to experience a longing for God's love and grace. For other people spiritual anorexia becomes intellectualized as various forms of atheism or agnosticism.

If you talk to people who are physically anorexic, you will find that they often experience food as dangerous, as a kind of toxin. In a similar way those of us who struggle with spiritual anorexia often experience spiritual nurture as dangerous or potentially toxic. For many years, Dale suffered from this form of spiritual anorexia.

> I used to go to church on Sunday morning, sit down, and check out. I could not have told you later in the day what was said in the sermon or which hymns we sang or anything else about the service. That kind of dissociation was not a conscious choice I made; it was just what happened. I have no doubt that I performed this vanishing act because at some level I experienced a threat and a need to protect myself. There was spiritual nurture available to me in those services, but I could not receive it. I responded as if an enormous danger were present, and I desperately tried to protect myself by disappearing spiritually, emotionally and mentally.

Resistance to spiritual nurture can be expressed also as ministry addiction. If we have given up on finding the spiritual nurture—the love and grace and intimacy with God that we need—we may conclude that our job in life is not to receive from God at all but rather to give to God. So we may focus our spirituality on giving to God in service. Although serving God is, of course, a good thing, people with spiritual anorexia sometimes try to cover up their inability to take in God's love by making extraordinary efforts to spiritually nurture others. However, like any effort to give away what we have not received ourselves, this strategy for life ends in exhaustion and resentment.

Dale spoke several years ago to a woman who had spent many years of her life serving the poorest of the poor. She had worked in AIDS hospices in Asia and with food distribution programs in a number of countries.

> I admired her dedication and her values. Her life was, for me, a model of a well-lived Christian life. In midlife, however, she found that her life was just not working, and she was deeply depressed. When we talked, she expressed confusion about how her life of dedicated service had not led to the spiritual maturity she had hoped for but rather to spiritual exhaustion, frustration and resentment toward God. She felt betrayed both by the mission group with which she was associated and by God. She confessed that she no longer felt that she was able to trust God. She had spent her life giving to God, and now she couldn't give anymore and she had no idea what to do with herself. The religious activities that once had sustained her, like praying for others or reading her Bible, were almost impossible for her. She felt completely cut off from God.

> It is tragic that this dear woman, as gifted and committed as she was, did not even consider the possibility that receiving from God was part of her vocation and calling. *Receiving* was not part of her spiritual vocabulary. When I asked her if she had found that her ability to receive from God had changed

over time, she had difficulty understanding what I was talking about. For her, God was a giver of good gifts—but only
to other people. As she understood it, her job was not to be
a recipient of God's generosity; it was, instead, to help God
distribute good gifts to others. So in the midst of an abundance
of God's grace and love, she was spiritually starving. She had
spent years denying her need to receive because being on the
receiving end seemed spiritually dangerous. It turns out that
she had come to the conclusion quite early in life that no one
would take care of her, no one would respond to her needs.
So, since it was basically hopeless to get her own needs met,
she had decided that things would work out better in life if she
focused on taking care of others. The result of this resistance
to spiritual nurture was exhaustion, depression and anger. And
over time, this toxic mix developed into spiritual anorexia.

Distorted self-concept. The second major characteristic of spiritual
anorexia is a profoundly distorted self-concept. People who are physically anorexic have very distorted physical self-concepts. If you hold
up a mirror to a person who is anorexic with respect to food, that
person may say, I'm fat. I'm way too big. I need to be smaller. The anorexic says this no matter how much objective information is available
to suggest that she or he is in fact not only smaller than normal but
smaller than is physically healthy. Often the language used to describe
the anorexic's physical self-concept sounds like, If only I could disappear, then things would be as they should be.

The same kind of profoundly distorted self-concept occurs in the
spiritually anorexic person. If you hold up a spiritual mirror to a person with spiritual anorexia, that person will say something like, It
would be better if I were smaller. It would be best if I disappeared

completely. Spiritual anorexics feel that they need to disappear to be safe in God's presence.

The anorexic will to disappear can unfortunately become confused with Christian teaching. Consider the following way of talking about the Christian message: "God is holy and cannot stand to be in the presence of sin. But we are sinful. So if we are in God's presence, we will be annihilated, because of the incompatibility of God's holiness and our sinfulness. Fortunately, Jesus stands between us and God. As a result, God doesn't see us."

In this understanding of the Christian message, the best thing is for us to be invisible to God. If this is how we understand the good news, we may find ourselves working harder and harder to disappear spiritually. And that is a pathway to spiritual death, just as working harder and harder to disappear physically leads to physical death. But is this way of talking about the Christian message really good news? Is "God can't see me" the best we can hope for?

Not even close. Jesus was very clear about this. The God of whom Jesus spoke searches the horizon looking for signs of the return of broken, damaged, missing-the-mark people like us. God is delighted when we become visible, when we can be seen. Jesus also taught that God is like a shepherd who searches for his lost sheep, and like a woman who lost a precious coin, hunts for it and then lights up with joy when she finds it (Luke 15:1-10). This does not sound anything like the god who can't tolerate being in the same room with us. The good news is that when God sees us, God's face lights up with joy!

Related to the anorexic's feeling of wanting to disappear is a fear of being a burden. To the person who is spiritually anorexic, it often feels shameful to have needs of any kind. Just as someone who is physically anorexic would prefer not to need food at all, someone who is spiritually anorexic would prefer not to have any needs for attention, support, help or love—from God or from others.

Juanita remembers a time when her own spiritual anorexia became apparent to her:

> One day when I was in my early twenties, I was having lunch with a close friend. She had been in a crisis for a few weeks, and I had spent many hours listening to her and supporting her. This was nothing unusual for me. I often gave in this way to others. But my friend said something that day that caught me off guard. "You are always here for me when I need you, but what do *you* need?"
>
> I was stunned. I never thought about having needs myself. I felt compassion for others in need, but I was unaware of having any needs of my own. My friend was inviting me to ask for something I needed, and I felt extremely uncomfortable. It scared me. I felt exposed and wanted to hide. I realized sometime later that I lived with the fear that if I needed something and asked for it, God would get upset with me and leave me. It was safer to disappear.

Control issues. The third common characteristic of anorexia is the presence of complex control issues. The main question for people who are physically anorexic often is: Who controls what goes into my body? Even the language suggests that boundary violations may lie near the surface of the anorexic's insistence on control. In the case of food anorexia there is often a significant connection between the anorexia and experiences of sexual boundary violations. In the case of spiritual anorexia there is a parallel connection between the spiritual anorexia and experiences of spiritual boundary violations. For example, it would not be too surprising if a person who was force-fed spirituality as a child developed spiritual anorexia as an adult. Spiritual anorexia is often an attempt to protect our spirits by setting extremely rigid boundaries around them. Rigid boundaries about spiritual things may protect us from spiritual abuse, but it can also cause our spirits to starve in isolation.

Another kind of control issue that is often a part of physical anorexia is the drive to control our bodies in an impossible quest for physical perfection. The underlying belief is that one's value is directly tied to having a perfect body. Anything less than perfection leads to deep feelings of worthlessness and self-loathing. In the same way spiritual anorexics can be driven by an impossible quest for spiritual perfection. The underlying belief is that we must be "good" (actually, perfect) to be close to God, because God will reject us if we are in any way short of perfect.

Some of us feel that we can't answer yes to the question, Are we good enough? until we are perfect. As a consequence we can get stuck in a kind of compulsive self-examination process that involves increasingly detailed interrogations about our behavior and motives. Sometimes called scrupulosity, this futile and unproductive quest is a sure sign that we serve a god who will reject anything less than perfection. Because a state of perfection can never be achieved, a person with this belief system never feels free to approach God or to receive the caring embrace from God that is our deepest longing.

HOW DO I KNOW IF I'M SPIRITUALLY ANOREXIC?

Here are some questions we can ask ourselves to assess whether we're suffering from spiritual anorexia:

- Do I have difficulty receiving from God?
- Do I have difficulty receiving from others?
- Do I experience despair in relation to my spiritual longings?
- Have I lost the capacity to experience spiritual longings or spiritual hopes?

- Am I trying to give away to others what I have not received my-self?

- Do I share the love of God with others but secretly doubt that God loves me?

- Am I accumulating resentments about the amount of energy I ex-pend on giving to others and how little I am getting back?

- Do I experience fear when I think about being close to God, even as part of me longs for closeness with God?

- Do I have rigid boundaries around my spiritual self in order to pro-tect myself from what I fear will be coercive or intrusive assaults by God or God's followers?

- Am I driven in my quest for spiritual perfection and unable to rest in receiving God's love?

If we answer yes to any of these questions, we need to take seri-ously the possibility that we are at risk for spiritual anorexia.

HOPE FOR THE SPIRITUALLY ANOREXIC

Let's return to Ted's story to see an example of what recovery might look like for people suffering from spiritual anorexia. When we left Ted at the beginning of this chapter, he was in church listening to a sermon about God's grace, but fearing that grace was dangerous and that it would result in a congregation that was passive and needy.

After the service Ted confronted his pastor and told him exactly what he thought of his sermon. The pastor knew about Ted's spiritual struggles from earlier conversations. He listened to Ted, acknowl-edged Ted's concerns and then suggested that Ted join one of the spir-itual direction groups even though he had some reservations about it. In spite of his reservations Ted decided to give it a try.

During the first meeting, the members of Ted's group shared about their personal lives and how they recently felt about their relationship with God. When it was Ted's turn to share, he asked if he could pass. Ted's pastor, who was a member of the group, said that he could, but asked if he would like to talk about why he didn't feel comfortable sharing. Ted explained that he was suspicious of this whole process and wasn't sure he trusted the other members of the group. The pastor thanked Ted for his honesty and for being willing to give the group a chance in spite of his hesitations.

After everyone had shared, the pastor led them in a reading of Scripture. He asked everyone to close their eyes, find a comfortable position in their chairs and relax. Ted tried to follow these instructions but found his anxiety rising. Then the pastor read the story in Mark 10 about Jesus inviting the children to come to him. After he had finished reading, the pastor asked the group to imagine themselves as the disciples in the story. "Why were they trying to keep the children from Jesus?" the pastor asked. In his mind's eye, Ted saw himself as the most energetic of the disciples, actively trying to keep the children away from Jesus. *Those children didn't know what they were doing,* Ted thought. Although the children were probably full of hope and expectation, Ted was convinced that keeping them at bay was protecting them from suffering the disappointment that was sure to come. *Christ was not Santa Claus; he was not going to just give them whatever they wanted,* Ted reasoned.

Ted's pastor read the story again. This time he asked the group to imagine themselves in the role of the children. Ted saw himself as the least enthusiastic of the children. While everyone else was running forward, he lagged in the back, telling the others that they were wasting their time. Ted expected to get rejected, and he felt justified in his cynicism when the disciples turned the children away. When Jesus invited the children forward, Ted stood his ground. *Let the other kids get their hearts broken if that's what they want,* Ted thought. He was going to stay in the back, where it was safe.

The pastor read the story one last time. This time he invited the group to see themselves sitting next to Jesus, welcoming the children. For a brief moment Ted saw himself in this way, looking at himself as a child. He saw the longing and the fear and, most of all, the shame in this child's eyes. He saw the shame of thinking that he deserved rejection, even as he longed to be embraced. It was terribly painful to see this, so Ted opened his eyes and worked hard to think of something else.

When the reading was done, some of the group members shared their experiences. Ted once again declined to share. Ted's pastor sent the group home with an assignment for the next week: They were to reflect on their private images of God. "When we get together next week," said the pastor, "we'll talk about how we see ourselves in relationship to God, and I want each of you to come back with a written list of at least two things you think you need from God."

Ted spent a few moments that night and some time in the parking lot before the next meeting thinking about the assignment. He was sure that God was good and was doing important things in the universe, but God didn't owe Ted anything. Ted thought that if he needed anything from God, it was to have no needs. When he wrote this down on a piece of paper, Ted had a vague feeling that there was something wrong with it, but he had no idea what it might be.

Other people in Ted's group named things they needed from God, and some had very long lists that reminded Ted again of children sitting on Santa's lap. One woman had two pages of things she needed from God, and it was all Ted could do to keep from laughing out loud at the woman. He was surprised to hear that one other person in the group had written exactly what he had written. She thought that she too needed to be not needy. When the pastor asked her why that was, she said that needing something from God felt too risky.

Over the next few weeks it became apparent to Ted that the god he served was a god who expected you to come bearing gifts and then lost all interest in you after that. Ted knew intellectually that this god was not consistent with the Christian story. In the group Ted and the other members were given the opportunity to formally renounce any gods-who-are-not-God they might be serving. One night, to the surprise of many, Ted stood before the group and said, "For most of my adult life I have served a god that always needs to receive and never gives back. Tonight, I renounce my allegiance to that god. I do not want to serve that god anymore. I will not serve a god who neglects his children."

While he was making this statement, Ted recognized a significant connection. As he spoke, he saw in a new way the similarity between his relationship with his neglectful god-who-is-not-God and the emotional distance, lack of nurture and impossible expectations that he had experienced as a child. He had expected to feel better somehow after renouncing his idolatrous attachment, but this observation was an extremely painful one and he left the group that night feeling worse than when he arrived. In the weeks that followed, Ted was consumed by resentments. During the day he was consumed by thoughts about how the god-who-is-not-God and his parents had harmed him, and those thoughts also kept him awake at night.

Members of Ted's group supported his renouncement and encouraged him to find a more positive relationship with God—or a more grace-filled God to have a relationship with. But Ted's resentments were powerful. He found it hard to even think about the possibility of a new relationship with God. After a few weeks of intense resentment, Ted was exhausted and depressed. He grew resentful of his pastor and the group for encouraging him along this path. He was certain that he was worse off now than he had been before he started the group experience.

One night Ted's pastor spoke about the importance of forgiveness. He described resentment, the pain it causes our spirits and the harm it does to us and to those around us. Ted found himself identifying with the description of resentment, but he was not ready to forgive. Even if it did hurt him, Ted couldn't imagine forgiving his parents or his god who was not God without a good reason to do so. Ted's pastor suggested that if anyone in the group had resentments, they might pray for God to give them insight and then stay open for an answer.

The group ended a few weeks later—on a sour note for Ted. He told his pastor and the group members that he regretted the whole experience and would not be attending their church anymore. Ted kept true to his word but started attending a weekly communion service at a church in a neighboring town. Months later, Ted reflected on his time at the spiritual direction group and decided he had learned something important from the experience. He knew now that he could not worship a god who was unable to nurture god's children. He was willing to admit that maybe there was a God who was different from his neglectful god-who-is-not-God. Maybe.

Ted saw his attendance at the weekly communion service as a kind of experiment. He liked the service because it was quiet and socially nondemanding. No one would interrupt his thoughts or try to cheer him up. And every service was a reminder that God loved to nurture his people. That's what the pastor said every week. It was a spiritual meal. God was providing food for his people. *Maybe,* he thought, *this God who loves to give spiritual nurture is real. Maybe.*

Then one Sunday, the pastor read aloud from the Gospel of Luke, and Jesus' words seeped through Ted's resentful fog: "Forgive them, for they do not know what they are doing" (Luke 23:34). For some reason this changed Ted's thinking just enough to make a difference. He began to see that his parents didn't know what they were doing when they raised him. They were doing the best they knew when they parented him; their own parents had been terribly abusive and, as a result, they didn't have any idea how to be nurturing parents. Ted began to see how his experiences at a very early age had shaped his image of God. It seemed important to acknowledge that his parents had not forced an image of God on him; blame was not an appropriate focus right now. Ted knew he had shaped his own god-who-is-not-God from his disappointment and his resentments. At the same time, Ted found himself able to acknowledge that he had neglected people in his own life without realizing what he was doing. He'd caused harm to friends and family in the past by doing exactly the kinds of things that so disturbed him about his parents and his god-who-is-not-God. This gift of insight humbled Ted.

Just then the pastor came to the part of the service where every week he said, "Thank you, God, for feeding us with spiritual food." Ted felt a wave of recognition wash over him. God had given him some important insights and even a readiness to seriously consider forgiveness—just like his previous pastor had said. And Ted hadn't even asked for it. This increase in his ability to forgive had come as a pure gift from God—the God who loves to spiritually nurture his people.

Ted heard from a friend at his previous church that just before Christmas week the spiritual direction groups were having a one-year reunion. Ted decided to go, even though he felt humbled to approach the group when he had left on such bad terms. When it was his turn to talk about how he was doing, Ted said, "A year ago I renounced the god I had served all my life. This led me into a spiritual wilderness. I was lost and confused. I know that I was resentful and I may have offended some of you. I'm sorry for that. When I look back now, I can see that God was nurturing me even then, giving me just as much grace as I could tolerate at the time. I'm doing my best to take in the grace that God is giving me on a daily basis. I don't know if I'll ever be really good at this, but I'm doing better now than I was last year. Thank you for being a part of my growth."

QUESTIONS FOR PERSONAL REFLECTION

1. To what degree do you relate to Ted's experience?

2. What experiences have you had that might make it difficult for you to receive nurture from God?

3. What has helped you receive good gifts from God and others?

4. Read the story in Luke 15:11-32, imagining yourself as the prodigal son. Let yourself take in all that your waiting father says and does in response to your return. Then reflect on this experience. What was it like for you?

5. Reread the story, imagining yourself as the older son. Let yourself take in what your loving father says to you. Then reflect on this experience. What was it like for you?

3

ADDICTIVE SPIRITUALITY

After beginning with the Spirit, are you now trying to attain your goal by human effort?

GALATIANS 3:3

Eric was raised by alcoholic parents. Because his home life was chaotic, Eric gravitated toward his neighbors, the Richardson family, whose lives seemed peaceful and orderly by comparison. One Sunday the Richardsons invited Eric to go to church with them. That morning as the choir sang their first hymn, Eric felt as if he had found his true home.

On subsequent Sundays, Eric was told that some of his actions were pleasing to God while others were displeasing. If he behaved properly, Eric would be pleasing to God. These fixed guidelines for behavior and the thought of clear, consistent responses from God were a great comfort to young Eric, whose home life was defined by shifting boundaries and unpredictable mood swings.

Years later when he was in his thirties, Eric woke up at five o'clock every morning and spent two hours reading and memorizing Scripture, and praying over a long list of prayer requests. He committed his evenings to several ministries at church, where he worked hard to please God.

Eric's morning prayer sessions and evening ministries left him exhausted. As a result, he performed poorly at work and was emotionally unavailable to his wife and two children when he got home at night. Eric's wife began losing her temper with him when he started falling asleep at the dinner table. The fights between them grew bitter, and Eric sought relief by attending extra church activities whenever possible. Although his religious performance was causing conflict in his life, Eric felt good that he was pleasing to God.

Then one day Eric's life collapsed. In the morning, he came downstairs from his prayer time to find his wife packing the car. She told him she was taking the kids to her mother's for the foreseeable future. "We never see you anyway," she said. At work that day, Eric was informed that his performance had been so poor that the company was placing him on strict probation: one more mistake in the next month and Eric would lose his job. Then, at church that night, Eric's pastor informed him and the rest of the missions board that Joe Clark, not Eric, would be receiving that year's "Most Valuable Pray-er" award for his hard work and dedication. "No one," said the pastor, "is as passionate about the Lord's work as Joe."

Eric went home to an empty house, crushed and defeated. The next morning he woke at five as usual, but found he could not get out of bed. Eric couldn't even manage to crawl out from under his blanket to call in sick for work that day. At ten o'clock a call came and Eric's boss left a message on his machine informing him that he had lost his job.

The next day Eric pulled himself together. Eric was going to do what he did best. He spent all that day reading Scripture and praying, not even pausing to eat. Work and family had been getting in his way. Now there was nothing to keep Eric from pleasing his Maker. But even with the extra effort, prayer and Bible study just didn't have the kick they once had.

Eric felt tired and empty. He had to spend an enormous amount of energy to be able to concentrate. Often he was distracted by feelings of resentment and self-pity. What was wrong with his wife? His boss? His pastor? Why weren't they behind him? Couldn't they see that he was doing God's work? Didn't that mean anything to them? When he dwelled on his resentments against his wife, Eric realized that he had been fighting with her from day one to get her to support him in the ministry he needed to do. He wondered if maybe she wasn't even a Christian.

When he wasn't distracted by resentments, Eric was overwhelmed by feelings of fear and guilt. How could he show his face at church when people knew his wife had left him? What if she wanted a divorce? How could a man of God suffer such a burden? Eric began to grow suspicious that perhaps God had abandoned him, and he began to obsess about what he might have done to displease his Creator.

After a two-day prayer binge, Eric was unable to move from the spot on the floor where he had fainted. After several hours he began to think about dying. It wouldn't be too hard to die, he thought. He just had to keep lying there, and dying might be the best thing for him now that he had lost God's favor.

Eric is a spiritual addict. His need for a spiritual "high" has driven him to extremes, and as a result he has lost his family and everything else he most valued in life.

The concept of addictive spirituality is hard for some people to grasp. How could something as important and as valuable as our faith become an addiction? Actually, anything that alters our mood in ways that we experience as pleasant has the potential for becoming addictive. Unfortunately, even good things can become addictive. Work addiction, sex addiction and food addiction are all examples of destructive relationships with good things. But what about *really* good things—things like worship, prayer and ministry? These things also can alter our moods in positive ways, and unfortunately, they also can become addictive.

Addictions to spiritual practices can be particularly confusing forms of addiction. They usually mask themselves as something else. Ministry addiction, for example, may look very much like commitment or dedication. Worship addiction can look like sincerity or devotion. But no matter how it looks to an outside observer, the inner life of an addicted person is very different from the inner life of a person who is committed, dedicated, sincere or devout. The difference between them is that while the highly motivated person is merely involved in his or her faith, the addict is using religious practices like a drug addict uses a drug.

Another example might help us clarify this point. Mike was an elderly man and a well-respected member of his faith community. He worked hard for his church and he felt obligated to be present at every meeting the church held. Mike was also a religious addict. One Wednesday his wife became ill with a severe stomach flu. At her age the danger of becoming dehydrated was significant, and she spent the day sleeping and sipping water. As she grew weaker, she needed her husband's help to move from the bed to the bathroom. Mike spent his day helping her and nursing a private sense of guilt. He knew that no matter how bad his wife's condition grew, when six o'clock came, he would have to leave her and go to the Wednesday night prayer meeting at church. His presence was not required at this meeting, nor was the meeting in any way significant to the politics or life of the church; it was simply the regular Wednesday night service. Still, Mike knew he would not be able to keep himself from going. He needed this religious ritual in order to function, in order to feel acceptable to God. When Mike missed any church service, he felt an enormous wave of guilt and anxiety. Six o'clock came and—even though his wife pleaded with him to stay by her side—Mike left his wife with a glass of water and walked out the door.

Something is seriously wrong here. Although the people at his church might see Mike as a dedicated and devoted Christian, his behavior is directly contrary to core Christian values and basic human decency. A prayer-meeting leader who has a sense of God's grace would have told Mike to go home to his wife. But Mike wouldn't have listened. Why? Because in his mind he can neglect his wife in the name of God. When we look at this story, we see all the signs of addictive spirituality—spirituality that has taken on the qualities of a full-blown addiction.

The stories of Eric and Mike may seem shocking or even hard to believe, but sadly, their behavior is nothing new. Neglecting the needs of others in order to satisfy addictive spirituality existed in Jesus' time as well. Luke tells the story of an expert in the law who interrogated Jesus, hoping to justify himself (Luke 10:25-37). This quest for self-justification is common among religious addicts. Jesus responded to this religious leader's question by telling him the familiar story of the good Samaritan. It is a story about a man who is beaten and robbed and left on the roadside to die. As the man calls out for help, two religious leaders, a Levite and a priest, hurry past him, paying no attention. Perhaps they were rushing to fulfill what they considered to be important religious obligations. Perhaps they were being scrupulous about the religious uncleanness that was associated with touching a dead body. If the man were already dead, or if he were to die while they were helping him, they would almost certainly have considered themselves unclean for seven days (Leviticus 21:1-2), and that would interfere with their religious practices. We have no way of knowing for sure whether these leaders were religious addicts. But their behavior is certainly consistent with religious addiction. They had something in their lives that was so important, so urgent, so demanding that it got in the way of helping a person in need. Jesus clearly sees their behavior as unloving. In contrast, he commends the behavior of a Samaritan who stopped to help the man—a person who would have been considered by most in Jesus' audience to be ungodly.

> On one occasion an expert in the law stood up to test Jesus. "Teacher," he asked, "what must I do to inherit eternal life?"
>
> "What is written in the Law?" he replied. "How do you read it?"
>
> He answered: " 'Love the Lord your God with all your heart and with all your soul and with all your strength and with all your mind'; and, 'Love your neighbor as yourself.' "
>
> "You have answered correctly," Jesus replied. "Do this and you will live."
>
> But he wanted to justify himself, so he asked Jesus, "And who is my neighbor?"
>
> In reply Jesus said: "A man was going down from Jerusalem to Jericho, when he fell into the hands of robbers. They stripped him of his clothes, beat him and went away, leaving him half dead. A priest happened to be going down the same road, and when he saw the man, he passed by on the other side. So too, a Levite, when he came to the place and saw him, passed by on the other side. But a Samaritan, as he traveled, came where the man was; and when he saw him, he took pity on him. He went to him and bandaged his wounds, pouring on oil and wine. Then he put the man on his own donkey, took him to an inn and took care of him. The next day he took out two silver coins and gave them to the innkeeper. 'Look after him,' he said, 'and when I return, I will reimburse you for any extra expense you may have.'

"Which of these three do you think was a neighbor to the man who fell into the hands of robbers?"

The expert in the law replied, "The one who had mercy on him."

Jesus told him, "Go and do likewise." (Luke 10:25-37)

The parable of the good Samaritan sums up Jesus' criticism of the priorities of the religious leaders of his time. Rather than attending to the needs of others, they were concerned primarily with meeting the demands of their own addictive spirituality. There is a second level to Jesus' story, however, in that it implies that there is something wrong with the religious leaders' understanding of who God is. When spiritual addiction is at work, there is almost always some form of distorted understanding about God at work in the addict's life.

The seed of spiritual addiction is often a drive to try to please God in hopes of earning God's love or favor. This is what Dale experienced as a young college student. He wanted to please God, but privately he feared this was impossible. Finding a way to please God seemed to be the only way to acquire God's love. But his sense of shame, the sense of being unpleasing, made the prospect seem hopeless. Because of Dale's fears and shame, God's grace and love—resources that were always, unconditionally available to him—seemed impossible to acquire, no matter how hard he tried. So he was driven to do more and more. When he started college, Dale could not miss church without becoming anxious and depressed. In fact, the only time he felt okay was when he was at church. As time went on he needed to attend church with greater and greater frequency to achieve a stable mood—to keep the feelings of anxiety and depression from becoming overwhelming. His increased attendance at religious services began to have a negative impact on his relationships and his performance in

school, but he continued to attend church as often as possible in spite
of the negative consequences. Though he thought of himself as simply
a dedicated and committed Christian, Dale was in the early stages of
a religious addiction.

Aspects of the spiritual life that can become addictive are not
bad things in themselves. Evangelism, religious ritual, prayer, Bible study, ethical conduct and all other aspects of spirituality have
value. But in the life of a spiritual addict, virtues are turned to
vices. When it comes to spiritual addiction, what looks like normal,
healthy, Christian behavior can actually be masking an extremely
destructive process.

WHAT IS ADDICTIVE SPIRITUALITY?

The word *addiction* can be defined in many ways. Some think of it
as a kind of idolatry. Addiction, according to this definition, is an
idolatrous attachment to the false god of drugs, work, sex and so on.
Unfortunately, defining *addiction* in this way can lead people to believe
that the only problem with an addiction is that it is focused on the
wrong object. If this were the case, then the solution to any addiction would be to replace the idolatrous attachment with an attachment
to God. Becoming addicted to spiritual or religious practices might
therefore seem like the solution to other addictions. But being addicted to these practices is still being addicted; the addictive process
is still at work in us. God desires a healthier relationship with us than
one that is distorted by the addictive process.

Addictive spirituality can be divided into three basic types: addictive doing, addictive feeling and addictive thinking. An addictive "doing" spirituality is one that is focused on a form of spiritual behavior,
such as evangelism, ethical practice, service or religious ritual. This
form of addictive spirituality is similar to work addiction, but it has an

additional veneer of spiritual language. Working addictively for God is still working addictively, and it is just as damaging as regular work addiction.

An addictive "feeling" spirituality is a spirituality that is focused on an emotional experience. The spectrum of emotional experiences that can become addictive is wide, ranging from shame and unworthiness to joy and elation. For example, we may find ourselves either working hard to feel bad about ourselves or working hard to feel happy about God all the time. Anytime we feel anything other than self-loathing or perfect love for God, we may get extremely anxious and do everything we can to get our desired emotions back.

An addictive "thinking" spirituality is a spirituality that is focused on the thrill that comes from being right. Believing that we have our doctrine exactly right can be an incredible rush. It allows us to see ourselves as the keepers of truth, and therefore as being closer to God than anyone else.

In all three forms of addictive spirituality, we focus on some aspect of the spiritual life because of the relief it provides us. The addictive object provides the addict with a special closeness to God. In the twisted logic of addiction we live as if *God accepts me because I do the right thing* (addictive doing), *God accepts me because I feel so bad about myself* (addictive feeling), or *God accepts me because I know my Bible inside and out and can take any wrong-thinking person down in an argument* (addictive thinking). This hoped-for closeness to God, because it is based on our performance, is fragile and tentative. People who are spiritually addicted live with a constant anxiety about whether they have done enough, felt enough or believed enough. Even as they look down on others who are not spiritually addicted in the same way that they are, they perpetually fear making a wrong move and falling out of God's grace.

CHARACTERISTICS OF ADDICTIVE SPIRITUALITY

Although all addictions are not the same, they have some common characteristics that can help us identify whether our spiritual lives are taking on addictive qualities. Every addiction demonstrates several qualities: tolerance, progression, withdrawal, compulsion, obsession and unmanageability.

Tolerance means that the same substance or behavior has to be used in increasingly larger doses to achieve the same effect. A gambling addict needs to take ever greater risks to get the same effect, and a spiritual addict needs more of the chosen spiritual process. If you find you have to place ever greater restrictions on your ethical conduct, pray for increasingly longer periods of time or win more arguments about theology, then you may be experiencing a tolerance effect in some area of your spiritual life.

Progression means that over any significant period of time, an addiction gets worse, not better. Not only do addicts "use" more; they also suffer more consequences, fall further out of sync with their own value system and become more willing to do whatever is necessary to get their next fix. A spiritual addict often becomes manipulative and abusive, loses friends and loved ones, and does things that stand in sharp contrast with the values of Christian spirituality. A compulsive evangelist, for example, may begin an addiction by simply talking with friends about faith issues, but eventually may lose a job because of being unable to go to the office water cooler without telling people that Jesus is the "living water."

Withdrawal is the reaction that addicts experience when they are deprived of the object of their addiction, and any kind of withdrawal is by nature uncomfortable. Just as heroin addicts who are taken off heroin suffer a physically painful withdrawal, spiritual addicts who are kept from engaging in their chosen spiritual activities suffer psychologically painful withdrawal. Spiritual addicts are extremely restless and irritable when not being able to go to church, read the Bible, tell people about Jesus, feel elated about salvation or win an argument.

Compulsion is a behavior that an addict cannot meaningfully control. Once alcoholics take a drink, they are completely unable to control or moderate their alcohol consumption. In the same way, once spiritual addicts begin to abuse an aspect of the spiritual life, they are unable to control or moderate their behavior. The spiritual addict who has to be right might know that getting into an argument with her husband is inappropriate, that criticizing his religious views will lead only to hard feelings between them, and that every other time she's started a fight the result has been disastrous. But once she says the first word to him, she can't help herself from getting fully embroiled in the debate.

Obsession is the experience of having our thoughts focused on one thing. Often, an obsession can be so powerful that it overrules our better reasoning and good intentions. For example, the sudden obsession to go to a strip club can be so overwhelming that all of a sex addict's reasons not to go to the club are set aside; he enters a sort of mental black hole where the consequences of addictive behavior are impossible to remember or don't seem to matter. For addicts of all kinds, obsession means that all their best efforts to stay clean and sober can be undone by a sudden, overpowering urge to use. People with addictive spirituality find their attempts to control, moderate and abstain from the object of their addiction are useless. Willpower is no power at all in the face of addictive obsession. Because part of addictive obsession is denial, spiritual addicts often really believe they are doing what God wants them to do. Their denial also makes them incapable of seeing the consequences of their behavior or admitting that it could really be a problem.

Unmanageability is the term used for the cumulative effect of addiction. As compulsion and obsession drive an addict's use, and as tolerance kicks in and the addiction progresses, an addict's life becomes increasingly unmanageable. Spiritual addiction leads to insane and destructive choices—like Mike's choice to leave his ill wife and go to church, and like the religious leaders' choice to walk away from a man who was dying. These are choices that an addict would not make if it weren't for the addiction. Relationships, work, basic self-care and normal tasks of daily living all become increasingly difficult and eventually impossible to maintain because of the addiction.

How Do I Know If I'm an Addict?

Usually we think of addictions as being about the improper use of negative things, like drugs. When an addiction is about something that is generally understood to be positive—like food, work, sex or spirituality—it is more confusing for us. For that reason, addictive spirituality is not always easy to see, especially in ourselves. Maybe we are active in our church and are deeply committed to its doctrine. Maybe we take prayer seriously and we pray a lot. Maybe we enjoy singing praise songs and listening to Christian radio. But does doing something a lot and enjoying it make us addicts? No, it does not. Spiritual practices are not addictive in and of themselves. Going to church, even going to church a lot, does not make someone a spiritual addict. Praying a lot does not mean you are addicted. Worshiping a lot does not mean you are a spiritual addict.

Jeff has a story that suggests how we might decide whether a certain spiritual activity is becoming addictive, based on the fact that addicts suffer when they stop "using":

> When I was a pastor, a woman who worked with a large campus
> ministry came to me for counseling. She came to me because

she knew I was a Christian counselor. Her concern was that she wasn't doing her daily devotions like she used to, and she wanted to get them back. She had been doing them forever. But one day she did the thing that everyone had always told her not to do; she missed a day. She had wrecked her streak. Then it got easer and easier to miss a day. Soon, she was hardly doing them at all anymore. She had tried, but she just couldn't get it right.

Because I sensed that an addictive process was at work in part of her spiritual life, I gave her the assignment to abstain from reading the Bible for two weeks, on purpose. After two weeks, we would see if she knew that she was okay just because of the love and grace of God—or if her sense of acceptance by God was dependent on the love and grace of God plus her religious performance. Religious performance can be very addictive, and sometimes one of the best ways to tell what's going on is to have a season of abstinence.

When addicts stop using, they become extremely agitated. They experience high levels of anxiety and become easily depressed. Addicts who have stopped using become irritable and can easily be provoked to actions that seem out of character for them. Many addicts isolate themselves when they aren't using, because they find it difficult to interact with people when they do not have their high. All the feelings that the spiritual fix was suppressing rush to the surface when the addict stops using, and he or she becomes highly volatile and sensitive. It is also common for spiritual addicts to switch addictions without realizing what they are doing. Spiritual addicts who stop abusing an aspect of their spiritual life may suddenly begin compulsively overeating, drinking or acting out sexually in order to compensate for the loss of their usual high.

If there is any question in our minds about whether we suffer from addictive spirituality, we can abstain from the aspect of the spiritual life that is the most compulsive for us and see what happens. If we are hooked on being right, we can stop asserting our views for a while and make an effort to see the point of view of others or even just listen without chiming in. If we are addicted to a spiritual behavior, we can stop that behavior for a period of time. If it is a spiritual feeling that we are hooked on, we can stay away from whatever it is that gives us that feeling. Then we can pay close attention to our mood and our reactions.

Here are some questions that might help us assess the extent to which the addictive process is playing a role in our spirituality:

- How comfortable am I when I abstain from a certain spiritual practice?

- Do I find myself unusually irritable, restless and depressed when I abstain from it?

- Do I find myself acting out in other ways?

- Do I begin to mentally obsess about the thing I have quit?

- Am I able to quit for as long as I promised? Or do I find myself coming up with an excuse for returning to the behavior before the period of time is over?

- Are other people telling me that my spiritual practices have done harm to our relationship?

- Has anyone ever said I'm "too spiritually minded to be of any earthly good"?

- Have I ever engaged in spiritual practices more than I intended?

- Has my commitment to spiritual practices ever gotten in the way of other important responsibilities?

- Over time have I found it necessary to gradually increase the frequency or intensity of my spiritual practices in order to feel less anxious about my relationship with God?

- Do I continue certain spiritual practices even though they leave me feeling depressed, anxious and frustrated?

- Does the very idea of taking a close look at my spiritual practices make me angry or resentful?

Positive answers to any of these questions might suggest that the addictive process is playing an unwanted role in our spiritual lives.

HOPE FOR THE SPIRITUALLY ADDICTED

There is hope for those of us who suffer from addictive spirituality. The painful recognition that something has gone wrong with us spiritually is the first sign that we may be ready to rebuild. It is recognizing our spiritual brokenness that puts us on the threshold of a new relationship with God. When we are able to face the truth about our distorted spirituality, we begin to develop the spiritual humility that is a necessary element in the foundation of a healthy spiritual life.

By way of example, we'd like to tell some more of Eric's story. When we left Eric, he'd lost everything he cared about and was preparing to take his own life. Fortunately, the thought of dying while being out of God's favor scared Eric into action. He got himself up off the floor and made a phone call to a relative. His Uncle Dennis had always been kind to Eric, and even though Eric hadn't seen him in several years, he was the only friendly figure in Eric's extended family.

Eric told his uncle about the events of the past week. Dennis replied that he wasn't sure what he could do for him, but that when he had been as desperate as Eric was now, he had found help in Alcoholics Anonymous. If Eric wanted to tag along, said Dennis, he'd take him to some meetings.

At his first AA meeting, Eric heard a man speak about God in a way that was completely foreign to Eric. This man, who introduced himself by saying, "Hi, I'm Bob, and I'm an alcoholic," talked about God as if God were compassionate and on our side. Bob seemed at ease, even peaceful, as he talked about his relationship with God. Eric didn't have language to understand it yet, but he could sense that Bob was not driven by fears about God or filled with shame about himself, even though Bob called himself an alcoholic. God did things for us, Bob said, and we didn't even have to earn those things. After the meeting, and at his uncle's suggestion, Eric asked Bob if they could meet sometime and talk. Bob gave Eric his phone number and said he could call anytime.

Reflecting on what Bob had said that night, Eric was startled to realize that he was serving a very different god from the one Bob served. Eric's god was demanding, impossible to please, dismissive and shaming. Though it frightened Eric to admit it, he had a growing feeling that he didn't want to serve this god any longer. However, this thought was immediately met with a deep fear and conviction that Eric's god must be disappointed in him for entertaining such an idea.

Even though the worship of this god had destroyed Eric's health, livelihood and family life, Eric was still very much under the control of a god-who-was-not-God.

When they met for coffee, Eric told Bob all about his troubles and his relationship with God. Bob listened intently. When Eric had finished, Bob said, "Well Eric, it sounds to me like you are full of fear and resentments. You've been trying to do for God what you need to let God do for you. I think you might need to scrap everything you think you know about God and start over. Sometimes the best thing to do is to start from scratch."

At home that night Eric felt even more alone than he had felt the day his family left him. He was actually considering parting ways with the only god he had ever known—the same god he thought had saved him from his alcoholic home. Eric knew from all his years of reading Scripture that Jesus had come to show us a God of love and compassion, a God who heals us and helps us. It seemed as if some of the people at the AA meeting believed in the God Jesus talked about, while Eric had been serving a harsh, impossible-to-please god. Eric was beginning to see that he was powerless over his relationship with his destructive god, and that worshiping this god had taken away everything he cared about.

Then Eric took the painful and grace-filled step of surrender. He decided he would no longer worship his god-who-was-not-God, and he prayed to the God of love and compassion whom he wanted to believe was out there somewhere, to rescue him from the fear and shame that were expressing themselves in his addictive spirituality.

The next morning Eric felt awful. It was Sunday, and Eric did not go to church. He had left his false god, and it felt to Eric that this required taking a break from all activity at his church, at least for a time. All the things that for him were connected to the worship of his old god were confusing, and Eric felt they needed to be temporarily removed from his life so that he could sort out what was helpful and what wasn't. This left a terrible, empty feeling inside him. Even though he didn't want to serve his not-God anymore, Eric felt strongly that his god had pulled away from him in scorn. Eric's perception of his god's absence was extremely painful. He began to fear that there might not be a loving God. Eric felt that he had committed an unforgivable sin and that he would soon be punished.

Without his mood-altering religious practices to numb him, the pain of the losses in his life was overwhelming. As Eric allowed this pain to surface, he felt for the first time the suffering of his fatherless children and the hurt of his neglected wife. He called Bob to ask if they could meet again.

When they met, Eric explained to Bob that he was letting go of his old ideas about God and that he felt empty and alone. "I'm still a Christian," said Eric, "but I don't have any idea how to live a healthy Christian life." Bob asked Eric if he thought it might be possible that there was a God who might actually love Eric and be willing to help him. After much reflection, Eric finally said, "I don't know."

"Well," said Bob, "are you willing to give it a try?"

Eric said he was willing but wasn't sure how to proceed. Reading the Bible, going to church, doing any kind of evangelistic activity and even praying felt dangerous to him. After more than thirty years of worshiping a god-who-was-not-God by those methods, Eric felt that they were not viable spiritual tools for him right now. Using these tools would almost certainly begin a compulsive cycle for Eric; they would dig him deeper into his addiction rather than help him out of it.

When Bob asked how he prayed, Eric replied that he started with a list of people who needed help and then told God what each person needed. Bob suggested that Eric try a new kind of prayer. Instead of handing God a to-do list and expecting God to carry out the instructions, Eric might sit quietly in the morning and see if God had anything to show Eric. If God had a to-do list for him, Eric might pray for the power to do just one thing on that list and then see what happened.

The next morning Eric got up at a reasonable hour and sat quietly. It felt as if very little was happening. He began to think about his wife and how much he had hurt her in the course of his addiction. The idea came to him that perhaps he should have a conversation with his wife in which he was honest about the harm he had caused, and then invite her to say whatever she wanted to say. Eric prayed for courage, called his wife for the first time since she had left and made an appointment to meet with her that same day.

The next time he saw Bob, Eric was elated. "I did what you suggested, and my relationship with my wife is beginning to change for the better." Bob reminded Eric that he had been looking for evidence of a loving God and that he had received exactly that. For the first time in a long time, Eric's spiritual life had been a source of grace rather than harm.

In continuing to practice this new form of prayer, Eric continued to receive guidance about the harm he had caused others and how to address it. After a bit of practice at this, Eric found himself being honest and humble in his relationships, and he became increasingly comfortable with telling the truth about his previous relationship with a god-who-was-not-God. Eric felt humbled by the years in which he had harmed people in active spiritual addiction, and he was grateful for a new experience of God.

When Eric thought back on all the professions of gratitude he had performed while on the worship team at church, they all seemed forced and unreal compared to how he felt now. Those professions had been fueled by an anxiety that had compelled him to express gratitude to his god or else his god wouldn't accept him. This new gratitude, however, felt different. It arose naturally from Eric's firsthand experience of grace.

Questions for Personal Reflection

1. In what ways do you sometimes find yourself trying to be "good enough" for God or trying to perform for God?

2. What problems has spiritual addiction created in your life or in the lives of people you know?

3. Read the story of the good Samaritan in Luke 10:25-32. Try to imagine yourself as the "expert in the law" (a theology scholar) to whom Jesus told the story, and then reflect on this experience. What was it like for you?

4. In what ways do you relate to Eric's struggles?

5. What can you take from Eric's story that might be helpful to you?

4

CODEPENDENT SPIRITUALITY

She came to him and asked, "Lord, don't you care that my sister has left me to do the work by myself? Tell her to help me!"

LUKE 10:40

When Alice heard that her brother was about to get a divorce, she sent him an e-mail telling him how wrong he was. Although she hadn't spoken to him in several years, she had a strong conviction that a Christian's duty was to remind others of what is right and wrong, and since her brother was a Christian, he should know better than to plan a divorce.

When she received no reply, Alice decided she had better put more effort into saving her brother from making a serious mistake. She did a little research and found what she thought was the best church close to her brother's home. She sent her brother another e-mail, recommending the church to him. Then she contacted the church and gave them her brother's phone number, asking them to call him because he was a Christian in trouble who was looking for a good church.

Alice was also spending a good deal of energy reminding her younger sister how to behave. Her sister had moved in with Alice and her husband after losing her job, and Alice was always aware of anything her sister did that was not quite right. Alice never failed to step in and confront her sister when she had crossed the line. Recently, Alice had been working very hard to get her sister to give up her relationship with a man who wasn't a Christian.

It wasn't long until Alice's sister announced that she couldn't stand living with Alice anymore, and that she was going to move in with her boyfriend. Before leaving, Alice's sister said, "If you are an example of what it means to be a Christian, then I don't want anything to do with it." Later that afternoon, Alice got word that her brother's divorce had been finalized. Alice was heartbroken and angry. She called her best friend for support, but to her surprise, her friend said, "Alice, all you do anymore is talk about other people. It is like your life is consumed by everyone else's spirituality instead of your own."

Alice hung up the phone in a rage. She spoke about the incident with her husband, who took the side of her friend and then said, "It's time for you to know this, Alice. I've only been going to church to please you, and I'm not going to do it anymore." Later that day, she began having dizzy spells. She felt that her life was falling apart all around her and there was nothing she could do about it.

Alice is spiritually codependent.

Like addictive spirituality, codependent spirituality can be confusing and difficult to detect. It often disguises itself as a deep concern for others, and people who suffer from it often say they are only behaving the way everyone behaves when they really love someone. However, spiritual codependency is not the same as love. It is a destructive form of spirituality that corrupts our love and concern for others. Although those of us who are spiritually codependent are unlikely to be aware of it, our "concern" for others may be little more than a strategy we use to try to control others.

Mark 10:17-22 tells a story about Jesus and a rich young man who comes seeking spiritual guidance.

As Jesus started on his way, a man ran up to him and fell on his knees before him. "Good teacher," he asked, "what must I do to inherit eternal life?"

"Why do you call me good?" Jesus answered. "No one is good—except God alone. You know the commandments: 'Do not murder, do not commit adultery, do not steal, do not give false testimony, do not defraud, honor your father and mother.'"

"Teacher," he declared, "all these I have kept since I was a boy."

Jesus looked at him and loved him. "One thing you lack," he said. "Go, sell everything you have and give to the poor, and you will have treasure in heaven. Then come, follow me."

At this the man's face fell. He went away sad, because he had great wealth.

Jesus looked around and said to his disciples, "How hard it is for the rich to enter the kingdom of God!" (Mark 10:17-22)

Something happens in this text that comes as a shock to those of us who are spiritually codependent: the young man walks away, and Jesus lets him go. He doesn't urge him to reconsider. He doesn't send his disciples after him to try to figure out some way for him to make a better choice. He doesn't shame him in an attempt to control his choice. He just lets him go. This kind of behavior is almost incomprehensible to spiritual codependents.

WHAT IS SPIRITUAL CODEPENDENCY?

In this chapter the term *codependency* means the obsessional focus on or attempt to control another person's mood or behavior. Normally, people talk about codependency in relationship to an alcoholic or an addict. For example, the husband of a drug addict, who spends all his time and energy trying to save his wife from her addiction, suffers from codependency. The symptoms of codependency have a remarkable parallel with the symptoms of addiction, but with one important difference. The addict's high depends on access to her drug or behavior of choice. When she has it, she's high; when she doesn't have it, she's low. The codependent's "drug" of choice is the addict. This means that when the addict is doing well, trying hard, making promises and showing improvement, the codependent's mood is high. When the addict is falling short, breaking promises, being inappropriate and relapsing into old patterns, the codependent's mood is low. In other words, the codependent's "addictive substance" is the addict, and the codependent can become as consumed with the actions and attitudes of the addict as the addict is with her drug of choice. And just as the addict is focused on keeping her substance in supply to ensure her ability to get high, the codependent is focused on keeping his substance (in this case, the positive performance of the addict) in good supply to ensure his own high. What this means, however, is that all the codependent husband's efforts to "help" his addicted wife are actually for the purpose of elevating, or keeping elevated, his own mood.

CHARACTERISTICS OF SPIRITUAL CODEPENDENCY

Spiritual codependency exists on a continuum from feeling anxious and responsible for someone else's spiritual well-being to believing that one can and should control other people. Codependent spirituality has a series of identifiable characteristics. By reading through this list of characteristics and honestly asking ourselves whether we share some of these characteristics, we can get a sense of whether we suffer from spiritual codependency or are at risk of becoming spiritually codependent.

Progression. Spiritually codependent behavior follows a progression similar to that of spiritual addiction. The spiritually codependent husband of a woman who isn't as interested in spirituality as he wants her to be begins simply by talking to her about God. Soon her relationship with God is all they ever talk about. Once this has become normal, he realizes that it isn't enough. He starts lecturing his wife about the moral and psychological consequences of her beliefs. This leads to long fights, and these also eventually become routine. Over time, he finds himself living in a constant state of resentment, spending his days building up ammunition against his beloved and then unloading both barrels as soon as she gets home at night. During these fights he starts to ask her point-blank whether or not she has been praying and reading her Bible. When she assures him that she has, he becomes possessed by a need to prove that she is lying. He begins invading her privacy by reading her journal and her e-mail, trying to catch her in a lie.

When they have reached the end of their progression, codependents exhaust themselves by trying to control what cannot be controlled. Spiritual codependents end up spiritually bankrupt and alienated from the loved ones they have tried to control.

Loss of self. Codependent spirituality often involves a loss of self. This form of destructive spirituality involves such a powerful focus on others that the spiritual codependent is not okay until others are okay. Jesus took note of this dynamic when he talked about people who had an obsession about the "speck of sawdust" in someone else's eye while ignoring the "plank" in their own (Matthew 7:3-5). Spiritual codependents are unable to focus on themselves and their own needs.

Lack of boundaries. Spiritual codependents usually have a poorly developed sense of interpersonal boundaries. They do not know how to set appropriate limits around their involvement in other people's spiritual lives. Spiritual codependents may believe that it is possible for them to "fix" other people spiritually, and they may act out this belief without ever pausing to reflect on the ethics of intruding on another person's relationship with God.

Attempts to control others. An emotional volatility usually accompanies spiritual codependency. The spiritual codependent can appear to be either meek or domineering. For example, a spiritual codependent might be meek and placating toward her spiritually addicted pastor, and then be domineering and even cruel to her family. Often, the spiritual codependent alternates between these two modes of control in the space of a few moments.

Resentment. Spiritual codependents are often resentful about the consequences of their spirituality. They are angry that their needs are not getting met, and they hold a grudge against others who they believe have forced them into the role of caretaker or messiah. Feeling that the world will fall apart if they don't step in to control other people, they get mad when people won't behave as directed. Trying to control other people's relationships with God is exhausting work— and resentments often flourish in the soil of exhaustion.

Fear is a common feature of spiritual codependency. First, spiritual codependents fear that if they give up codependent spirituality, people will be harmed spiritually. In spite of an abundance of evidence that compulsive efforts to help others are either ineffective or counterproductive, spiritual codependents may still insist on continuing these efforts. What would happen if they stopped? The fear is that all hope would be gone, that the worst would happen. The fear is that no one else could manage this situation better than we are managing it. That is probably the central fear—that no one else is available to do what needs to be done. Spiritual codependents are on their own. This fear may be rooted in a belief that God is so impotent and disinterested that they must step in and do God's work. Spiritual codependents have to meddle with other people's relationships with God because they are convinced that God is not capable of working on that relationship without their added pressure. Unfortunately, by acting on these beliefs, they are placing themselves in God's role, and in the process they often interfere with the work of God's Spirit in people's lives.

The second fear about giving up codependent spirituality is that our own spiritual lives will become passive, disengaged and uninvolved. Spiritual codependents fear that because there will be so little for them to do, they will become self-focused, self-centered. The codependent husband of a drug addict usually cannot imagine what life would be like without his obsessive focus on his wife's addiction. He is running so fast on the treadmill of codependency that he can't imagine anything other than running faster. Similarly, the spiritually codependent person may find it difficult to imagine what life would be like without the familiar obsessional efforts to control another person's spirituality. The fear is that stepping off that treadmill will lead to disaster. Who will I be if I don't have other people's problems and spiritual needs to obsess about? The fear is that nothing of value will be left, that life will be empty.

Spiritually abusive behavior. Codependency can easily become abusive when the codependent is in a position of power. Pastors, teachers and other individuals who feel the need to control the spiritual lives of those who look up to them run a high risk of becoming spiritual abusers. They are likely to say and do things that are shaming, controlling and disempowering in their misguided attempts to help others.

THREE TYPES OF SPIRITUAL CODEPENDENCY

We can act out our spiritual codependency in relationship with spiritual addicts, with nonaddicts and with God. We'll look at each of these relationships as a distinct type of codependent spirituality, because certain qualities are unique to each of these relationships.

Codependency in relationship with an addict. In chapter three we told the story of Mike, the spiritual addict who had left his dangerously ill wife at home alone while he went to a prayer meeting. What we left out of that story were the perspective and actions of Mike's wife, Peggy. She later apologized to her husband for begging him to stay home with her. She admitted that she was wrong, that the church is indeed more important than her temporary illness. She asked his forgiveness and promised not to act that way again. Peggy knows from long experience that her husband stays in a good mood only as long as nothing comes between him and his church meetings. But because this leaves her feeling resentful, she also finds opportunities to complain to her children in a joking way about her husband's behavior, often in front of her husband. Peggy is what we call an "enabling" codependent. She supports her addicted husband's behavior by helping him get what he wants.

The codependent person who loves a drug addict often tries by any accessible means to stop the addict's behavior. However, the codependent person who loves a spiritual addict is more likely to take on an enabling role as Peggy did, and place the addict on a pedestal, believing that the addict is a spiritually important person because of the obsessive religious activity.

Codependency in relationship with a nonaddict. Codependency is not limited to relationships with addicts. Codependency, as we have defined it, is any obsession to control another person's mood or actions, and this includes spiritual moods and actions. Whenever we experience an unmanageable obsession to control another person's spirituality, we suffer from spiritual codependency. An example might help to illustrate how codependent spirituality is acted out in a relationship with a nonaddict.

Ann lives with a constant sense of guilt about her adult son, Jerry. Jerry doesn't go to church, he doesn't read his Bible, and Ann suspects that he doesn't even pray. When she thinks about Jerry's spirituality, Ann experiences an enormous amount of stress and worry. She simply cannot live with the idea that she, the daughter of a well-known pastor, could have raised a nonbelieving son. Sometimes she is so ashamed that she can hardly bring herself to go to church.

Ann spent years visiting Jerry but typically gave little attention to his children, her grandchildren. Instead, because of her religious anxiety, all her attention was on Jerry. She often began their visits with a series of questions. When was the last time he prayed or opened his Bible? Had he been going to church? Did he read the Christian books she had sent him? Following her interrogation, Ann often spoke about Betty, Jerry's older sister. What a wonderful child Betty was! Did Jerry know that Betty was always in church with her on Sundays and prayed for her mother's health every night? She couldn't have asked for a more perfect child than Betty. When she finished these guilt trips, Ann started in on the bribes. Did Jerry want her to baby-sit? She was willing to come over on Friday nights so he could go to a new Bible study at her church. It would be a big sacrifice for her to give up going herself, but it was more important that he go.

As it became clear to Ann that these visits were not working and were only increasing her anxiety and grief, she decided to cut Jerry out of her life. For a year she didn't call him or visit. She still managed to interrogate, guilt-trip and bribe him indirectly through Betty, but she never made any attempt to see him or his children. After a year, when this strategy hadn't paid off, Ann switched back to her former, more aggressive strategy and went into a frenzy, calling Jerry or dropping by unexpectedly multiple times each week. These episodes ended when Jerry asked her to leave his house and not return.

People like Ann defend their behavior by saying they are simply doing what any loving and concerned parent would do. They reason that the consequences of being wrong about spiritual matters are so great that the only sane thing to do is to use every possible means to rescue the loved one who is in jeopardy. What Ann doesn't realize is that her assaults on her son's spirituality are not motivated by love but by her own deep anxiety. Love does not ask us to control another person. Fear and shame fueled Ann's attempts to control her son. Even worse, her efforts to control her son's spirituality actually drove him further away. Ann spent years neglecting her grandchildren and trying to manipulate her son, all in vain. If she had accomplished anything, it was only that she had created a painful division in her family.

In spiritual codependency, we become like Ann; we make ourselves responsible for someone else's spiritual well-being. Once we feel this responsibility, we also feel justified to (or even driven to) meddle with the other person's relationship with God. But codependency can also be directed toward friends, spouses, coworkers, fellow church members and even complete strangers.

Codependency in relationship with God. Spiritual codependency can also affect our relationship with God. For example, if we mistakenly believe that we have the power to control God's mood, our relationship with God can become distorted. When we think we are that powerful, either we work to the point of exhaustion in an attempt to make God happy or we are thrown into turmoil when we do the things we believe have the power to make God sad. But this god is not God at all. This god apparently has such poor emotional boundaries that its mood swings in response to our every thought and action. In spite of how little sense this makes, many people tiptoe through their Christian lives doing everything they can to prevent this god from having a negative mood swing. The fear is that this god's mood will suddenly swing toward anger and unforgiveness. For those of us who cannot let go of a relationship with this kind of not-God, the spiritual life becomes a frenzy of anxiety and resentments as we try to think and feel and do just exactly the right things to keep this volatile god's mood out of the danger zone.

Thankfully, our behavior does not control God's mood, and so we need not spend our spiritual lives becoming exhausted in the effort to make God happy. This does not mean that the things we think, feel and do are not important to God, as if God were remote and emotionless. To understand how this works, it might be helpful to think about a healthy parent-child relationship. When a young boy does something to please his mother—like drawing her a picture—he is not attempting to manipulate his mother's mood or to save himself from her anger. The boy is giving expression to a love that already exists, and his mother's joyful response is not controlled by her son's actions but is an expression of the same preexisting love. By giving and receiving, they are affirming the love they share.

When the same boy does something that upsets his mother, like throwing a tantrum, she might be angry or upset or impatient. And these emotions may seem at first to be something caused by her son. He did something, and now she is angry. But being a good parent, she knows that she needs to respond to both her anger and her son's behavior. As she takes responsibility for her own emotions she finds herself increasingly able to focus appropriately on what her son's tantrum means. She analyzes the situation to discover what her son might need to learn and how she might help him grow. Notice that whether her son is on his best behavior or worst behavior, the mother's love remains constant. Like a good parent, God does not depend on our doing good things to be happy. Nor does God respond to our bad behavior with anything less than love. Whether we are on our best behavior or our worst behavior, we remain the precious, lovable, fallible children of a God of love.

HOW DO I KNOW IF I'M SPIRITUALLY CODEPENDENT?

Here are some questions that can help us assess our risk of being spiritually codependent:

- Do I often find myself anxious about another person's spiritual well-being?

- Do I feel personally responsible to "set people straight" about their beliefs or actions?

- Am I attempting to control someone else's spirituality?

- Do I make excuses for myself when I intrude on someone else's spiritual life, telling myself that it is for their own good?

- Have I lost my sense of where my own spirituality ends and another person's relationship with God begins?

- Do I harbor deep resentments against others for not following my spiritual advice?

- Am I at risk of disempowering others by using my position of authority to exert undue influence over their relationship with God?

- Has anyone ever said (or hinted) that my efforts to be helpful spiritually were disrespectful or shaming?

If we can answer yes to any of these questions, we may be at risk of at least one of the three types of codependent spirituality.

HOPE FOR THE SPIRITUALLY CODEPENDENT

For those of us who are spiritually codependent, it may be hard to imagine a noncontrolling way of being involved in the spiritual lives of others, but as with abusive, anorexic and addictive spirituality, recovery is possible. Later in this book we give more specific information about how the recovery process works. For now, it might be best to consider an example of what recovery looks like by returning to Alice, the "raging" spiritual codependent we introduced at the beginning of this chapter.

Alice felt like her life was falling apart. Her next move was to call another friend and say the obvious, "I feel like my life is falling apart." "Maybe it is," said her friend, and then she recommended a Christian counselor who had been helpful to a family member. Alice agreed to make an appointment with the counselor.

Alice spent her first session of therapy talking about all the people in her life who didn't appreciate how helpful she was being and how angry she was at them for not doing what was right. At the end of the session the therapist said that the session had been helpful to her in getting clear about everyone else's problems, and that in the next session they would talk about Alice. The therapist sent Alice home with an assignment: to start a prayer journal. Every day of that week she was to write down her own thoughts and feelings, excluding any description or discussion of other people's problems.

When carrying out her assignment, Alice was surprised by how much anger she began to feel toward God. Her journal pages quickly filled with complaints that God was not correcting her brother, her sister or her husband. She also had concerns about several other people in her life that God was not addressing. Alice was really mad. Why was God leaving all the work to her? She was really tired and felt it was about time for God to take action.

In talking with her therapist about the assignment Alice realized that the god she was serving was an extremely weak, passive and irresponsible god. Alice's god was so irresponsible that Alice felt she had to do all the work to keep other people's lives from falling apart. When she said this out loud, Alice's therapist said, "Alice, it sounds like you are trying to do God's job."

Alice's reply came out before she knew what she was saying: "Somebody has to."

Over the next several sessions Alice began to realize that she had taken on God's job in the lives of others and had failed miserably at trying to fix them. "I can't do it. I wanted to help people, but I've only made a bigger mess," Alice said to her therapist. With her therapist's help, Alice was gradually able to step away from her job of playing God, but she felt as if she were leaving the post vacant.

During this process Alice suffered horrible anxiety attacks. When she saw a loved one act in a manner that she felt was wrong, Alice felt as if her world were coming apart at the seams. She had to be reminded frequently by her therapist and her friends that life had not been working so well when she was in charge of the universe. In one of her moments of panic Alice called a friend who told her, "By not controlling things, you are testing to see if there really is a God who will step in and help you. Even though it's scary, isn't it worth a shot?"

Alice's therapist suggested that Alice meditate on Psalm 46:10: "Be still, and know that I am God."

She encouraged her to pray for eyes to see where God was active in her own life and in the lives of those she loved. After some time—and not a few relapses—Alice was increasingly able to surrender her frantic efforts to control other people. She discovered that she herself had more than enough issues to work on as she sought to rebuild her own badly damaged spiritual life.

Eventually, Alice called her sister and asked if they could meet for coffee. Her sister reluctantly agreed. Over coffee, Alice told her sister, "I realize I've been trying to play God in your life and I'm sorry. I'm learning about what I can and can't control, and how disrespectful my behavior has been." After that meeting Alice's sister started dropping by the house, and Alice interacted with her sister on new terms.

Alice asked how she was doing, invited her to stay for dinner if she liked and never interrogated her about her relationship with her boy-friend or anything else about her personal life. She just let her sister be herself and feel at home. This was often difficult for Alice, and she had many anxious moments during her sister's visits, but she prayed through them and was given the strength to be a new kind of sibling to her sister.

Alice also sent her brother a new e-mail. She said to him more or less what she had said to her sister—that she had been wrong in trying to control him and that she hoped to behave differently in the future. This time, Alice got a reply. It was just two words: "Thank you."

A week later Alice received a longer response. In this e-mail, her brother said, "Your email stunned me. I didn't think you were ca-pable of writing a letter that didn't try to guilt-trip me or shame me. I don't know what happened to you, but the only thing I can think of is that maybe God is changing you. I thought that God was like the old you—controlling and shaming—but this is beginning to change my mind."

Alice's willingness to be weak and wrong instead of controlling led to the kind of change in her brother that she had been trying to cre-ate by force. Alice was struck by both the grace and the irony of that discovery. "Maybe this is a sign," Alice told her therapist, "that God really will step in when I get out of the way."

The next Sunday at church Alice heard in a new way something she had heard many times before: "My yoke is easy and my burden is light" (Matthew 11:30). Alice sensed that Jesus was inviting her to come to him and rest. In that moment she was filled with joy and hope. While there was still much that she felt uncertain about, she now felt assured that God was present and active and didn't need her to fix everyone around her. In fact, God would heal Alice and let her rest. For the first time in her life, Alice allowed herself to rest in the knowledge of God's love and grace.

QUESTIONS FOR PERSONAL REFLECTION

1. What fears and anxieties do you experience about other people's spiritual well-being? How do these fears and anxieties affect your behavior?

2. Read the story in Mark 10:17-22, putting yourself in the place of one of Jesus' disciples who is listening to this dialogue. Then reflect on your experience. What was it like for you?

3. Reread the story, putting yourself in the place of the rich young man who comes to Jesus and then walks away. What was this experience like for you?

4. What does it mean for you, in practical terms, to entrust those you love to God's care?

5

DISTORTED IMAGES OF GOD

Our real idea of God may lie buried under the rubbish of conventional
religious notions and may require an intelligent and vigorous search
before it is finally unearthed and exposed for what it is. Only after an
ordeal of painful self-probing are we likely to discover what we actually
believe about God.

A. W. TOZER

The first step in rebuilding a damaged spiritual life is to thoroughly assess the extent of the damage. This is an absolutely critical step in any spiritual reconstruction project. We need to ask, How deep is the problem we are up against? and, How badly damaged is the building we want to repair? Reconstruction should begin only after a thorough assessment of the damage to the existing structure and its foundation.

Destructive spiritual patterns like abusive, anorexic, addictive and codependent spirituality usually signal that the problems we are facing are foundational problems. Something about our spiritual foundation—our relationship with God—has been badly damaged. If this is the case, then the rebuilding process must begin at the foundations. Rearranging the furniture won't help. A new coat of paint won't do the trick. Adding more supports to our structure will be a waste of time if our foundation isn't solid. In fact, we may even need to clear away some significant portions of the existing structure before the foundations can be thoroughly examined and repairs can be made. There is no way to know at this stage how much, if any, of our current spiritual structure can be preserved. That will need to wait until we have made repairs to the foundation.

UNDERSTANDING THE PROBLEM OF GODS-WHO-ARE-NOT-GOD

It is our conviction that foundational spiritual problems—damage of the kind we have been talking about—comes from living in relationship with gods who are different from the God of love and grace who has been revealed to us in Jesus. We have been living in relationship with false gods, idols—usually small, petty, vindictive, impotent, angry, weak and unforgiving idols—that we have constructed for ourselves out of our experiences of resentment, disappointment, fear, pain and shame.

To understand how idolatrous attachments work, we need to recognize that the God of our convictions, the God of our formal theology, can be quite different from the God of our experience. Our formal theology is what might appear on a statement of faith. But this is not necessarily what shapes our behavior in ordinary life. We can see this clearly in the contrast between our private fears about God and our formal beliefs about God. Our formal theology probably contains affirmations such as "God is love" or "God is patient." We believe these things to be true. If we had to take a quiz about God's character, we would have the right answers. If we were asked, Is God loving? we would answer yes. That's our formal theology. But formal theology, while important, is not all there is.

We all know how easy it is to believe that God is love and yet to have no practical access to this love in our daily lives. It may be that God is, for us at least, only theoretically a loving God. Our fears about

God may crowd out or compete with our formal beliefs about God. Sometimes in an instant our subjective experience of God can shift from a God who is love to a very different image—perhaps to a god who loves us only if we perform well or to a god who doesn't even like us, much less love us. Similarly, we may be convinced that God is full of grace, but the god of our experience can still be abusive, temperamental, unreliable, passive or distant. Even though we believe, as Scripture teaches, that love "keeps no record of wrongs" (1 Corinthians 13:5), we may fear that God spends all day, every day, doing exactly that—keeping a list of our every impure thought and unkind deed. Even though we may believe that God is patient, we may feel that God has abandoned us because we continue to struggle with long-established character defects.

A good example of the difference between our formal theological convictions and our real spiritual commitments comes from Juanita's experience in co-leading a church-based cancer support group for many years. Over time it became evident to the group that the response of group members to being diagnosed with cancer revealed something important about their real experience of God.

All of us in the group believed that God is a God of love and grace, not a God who punishes people by giving them cancer. The people who attended the group would all have affirmed this. But the truth is that some of us lived with deep fears about God. Some people came into our group in a depression, feeling that God had abandoned them. Some thought they had developed cancer because they weren't good enough spiritually or because they were being punished for something they had done. Others felt that God had let them down—that God was too passive to be of any real help to them during this crisis. Not everyone joined the group in a state of spiritual trauma; some experienced an ongoing sense of God's loving presence throughout their experience with cancer. But most group members discovered that their medical crisis offered some insight into their deepest beliefs about God.

Although formal theology has its place, it is not always as helpful as we would like when we are struggling to rebuild a badly damaged spiritual life. When we are doing a major spiritual rebuilding project, we almost certainly need to focus our attention on the images of God that inform our daily lives. Those images often reveal a great deal about what our central spiritual commitments really are and how closely we are attached to gods-who-are-not-God. If we have built our spiritual house on a foundation of distorted images of God, we have built on sand. To enter into a relationship with the living and true God, we must tear down our existing spiritual home, demolish the foundation and start anew. But before we take such drastic action, we need to assess the damage to our foundation by looking at our distorted images of God.

IDENTIFYING SOME COMMON DISTORTED IMAGES OF GOD

We all carry within us a variety of images of God. Images are not concepts or abstract ideas but more like powerful pictures. Our images of God tend to be highly personal. We all form our own images of who God is based on our unique life experiences. As a result there is probably no way to catalog all the possible images of gods-who-are-not-God. However, there is a short list of distorted images that occur with great frequency. The list that follows is not exhaustive, but it can give you a sense of some of the not-Gods that compete for our loyalty and service. Many people experience more than one of these false images.

If you recognize your own experience as you read these descriptions, we want to remind you that the God of love and grace revealed to us in Jesus desires to free us from our distortions so that we can come to rest securely in the truth that we are loved.

The abusive god. Those of us who live with an image of God that is abusive live under the rule of a petty tyrant. An abusive god is almost always quick to anger and slow to forgive—which is, of course, exactly the opposite of the God of Scripture, who is "compassionate and gracious, / slow to anger, abounding in love" (Psalm 103:8).

Often this god-who-is-not-God is angry—usually for reasons that have not been explained to us or that we don't understand. This god tends to be unapproachable, impulsive, violent, cruel and even sadistic, so we can never be sure if this god is angry or if we are in danger. When we are attached to a god of this kind, we feel that we may be subjected to divine wrath at any moment; one false move and we can expect to be harshly punished. This false god carries a club and isn't afraid to use it. When bad things happen to us, we are sure we are being punished. When good things happen, we are afraid to enjoy them too much out of fear that our god will take the good things away to punish us for enjoying them too much. When our spiritual foundation is built on a relationship to an abusive god, we find it difficult to allow ourselves to enjoy any part of life without fear of repercussions.

Jeff grew up under this kind of fear and spiritual tyranny that is rooted in an image of an abusive god. Jeff's god was constantly pointing a critical finger at him, finding fault with him for even the most minor of failures or misdeeds. Jeff felt that he had to "get it right" all the time "or else." The "or else" part was a threat that was never fully clarified, but he didn't want to risk it. Jeff felt that he had to believe exactly the right doctrine and behave exactly according to the code his church taught or he was in danger of being rejected by God.

When we serve an abusive god, we are filled with fear and shame. We might not acknowledge this, but it is a powerful force in our lives. We may find ourselves sometimes hiding from this god, and at other times we try to placate god by working endlessly to be, think and feel right in order to avoid punishment. Of course, we may be so accustomed to this fear and shame, and these efforts to please, that they feel normal to us. But the fear and shame generated by an abusive god may drive us to addictively do more and more for our god, altering our mood while we act like slaves. Or our fear and shame may leave us in anorexic despair. In an attempt to protect ourselves and others from the harsh, punitive god we serve, this fear and shame can also lead to abusive or codependent attempts to control ourselves and the actions and beliefs of those we love.

The abandoning god. If we are idolatrously attached to an abandoning god, we may feel that God either has left us completely or is present but continually threatening to leave us at the slightest provocation. Being abandoned, we live in a kind of spiritual vacuum. We are totally alone and cannot perceive any love or grace at work in our lives. The little good we do see in our lives has come by chance and probably won't last. Convinced that we are on our own, we act as though we must fend for ourselves.

Having a god who is present but constantly threatening to leave leads to a life of anxiety. This god is not committed to us for the long haul but is waiting for us to misbehave, and when we do, we deserve abandonment. The abandoning god may grow impatient and leave us for no reason at all. In a state of constant fear of abandonment, we try to do anything in our power to keep our god from leaving. When we don't feel close to this god, we panic and fear the worst. If we do feel close to god, it is not a restful experience because we fear that we will be abandoned at any moment.

When Juanita first sought counseling, a powerful image came to her. She saw herself as a small child in a large crowd of people, and God was holding her hand. In the image she started to talk about the distress she was experiencing, but at that moment God pulled his hand away and disappeared into the crowd. She was left alone and lost in a crowd of people she did not know. For Juanita this distorted image of God was closely connected with a belief that she deserved to be abandoned.

Those of us who serve an abandoning god try hard to perform well so we won't be left alone. Although we may have moments of feeling close to this god, these moments of closeness are fleeting, insecure and contingent on our good behavior. When our god is at a distance, we interpret this as an appropriate response to us because we are irreparably damaged spiritually. We may conclude that no matter how hard we try, closeness with this god is not possible.

The emotionally distant god. An emotionally distant god does not care about our emotional needs. This god has more important things to attend to than our emotional problems. This god has a whole universe to look after, not to mention the people on this planet who are worse off than we are. This god notices only when eagles fall, never sparrows. Some who serve this god make excuses for their neglectful deity: "There are millions of people worse off than I am, so my problems aren't so important after all." But making excuses does not give us any real comfort or help. The emotionally distant god is not just distant but also emotionally aloof. This deity is uncomfortable around any kind of emotional expression. When we are experiencing emotional difficulty, this god demands that we snap out of it and move on. Or we should go to our room and not come out until we have a smile on our face. There is no possibility of receiving comfort from an emotionally distant god. A foundation built on a relationship with such a god prevents us from knowing the God who understands and cares about our emotional well-being.

As a missionary kid Juanita was actively aware of the needs of others in the world. She had a sense that others' needs were more urgent and more important than her own. As a young adult she realized that this idea had translated into a distorted image of herself in relationship to God. She saw herself at the end of a very long line of people, waiting for some attention from a preoccupied god. This not-God was too busy with everyone else's needs and did not have the time or patience to attend to her emotional needs.

When we serve an emotionally distant god, we are likely to experience shame because our needs and feelings do not matter. In fact, our needs and feelings become a problem to us and to god. As a result we may deny or minimize our feelings, effectively removing them from our awareness. What may seem to matter instead is having right doctrine and behaving well. Intimacy with this divine being is impossible, and ultimately we do not matter to this god. If we serve an emotionally distant god, we may find ourselves serving others while denying our own need for God's love and grace. Eventually we become exhausted and resentful, and we find ourselves lacking compassion for the people we are trying to serve.

The passive god. A passive god cannot help us in our time of need. We may see god as powerful but not active in this world and not coming to the aid of people. Thus the passive god may be uncaring. Or we may see this god as impotent, lacking the power to be of assistance. This god is unreliable, offering no practical help, so we have to rely on ourselves.

Several years ago a pastor told Dale that his compulsivity in ministry—his ministry/work addiction—was connected to his relationship to a passive and impotent god-who-is-not-God. Since this not-

God was not powerful enough to be very helpful, it fell to this god's followers, especially pastors, to do the heavy lifting in ministry. And so the pastor worked hard to pick up the pieces that god couldn't handle. As he reflected on the possible origins of his experience of God as passive and impotent, he identified a specific event. When the pastor was a teenager, his best friend was killed in a car accident, a traumatic loss for him. He now realized that he had concluded after the accident that God could not be both loving and powerful. So, since he wanted to believe that God was loving, he concluded that God must not be very powerful. The pastor did not develop his image of God through a long, dispassionate, theological deliberation, but through a traumatic experience. As he talked further, it became clear that his image of God was also shaped earlier in life by his relationship with his father—a distant, passive figure who never offered him any support, help or protection. From these life experiences the pastor developed a deep fear that God is passive and impotent, unable to help when we most need help.

When we serve a passive god, we feel unprotected, vulnerable and alone. Self-reliance may seem like our only choice. Though we may be angry with this god, we would probably never express our anger openly. And as we try to do for others what our god seems unwilling or unable to do, we may also become angry with them. In addition, we are likely to experience shame because we believe we do not deserve love or care. Some of us who have served this kind of god have worked very hard to compensate for god's passivity, which may be a source of embarrassment to us. As a result, we may drive ourselves to exhaustion.

The god of impossible expectations. The god of impossible expectations is never pleased with us, no matter how good we are. We may feel that if we don't do everything we are asked to do at church, if we don't read our Bible and pray enough, or if we don't behave according to the rules, god will be disappointed with us. Even though we are doing everything we possibly can to please god, we feel that this god is still not happy with us. This god always and eternally withholds approval. As a result, we probably find little "good news" in our spiritual experience. Our spiritual activities are likely to lead to spiritual exhaustion, resentments, bitterness and despair.

Spiritual exhaustion and despair characterize much of what Dale experienced while serving a god who was impossible to please. The personal image that Dale carried with him was of a god who was always sadly shaking his head in disapproval and disappointment. Spiritual life was like sprinting toward a goal, except that as soon as Dale got close, god would move the goal a little farther away. Reaching the goal was impossible. Dale's rewards were exhaustion and frustration, no matter how endlessly he worked to please his god.

When we serve a god of impossible expectations, we also experience the shame of spiritual failure, which can lead to mood swings from despair to frantic efforts to achieve perfection. Our periods of despair may leave us spiritually anorexic, feeling too exhausted and hopeless to keep striving for the impossible. Our times of perfectionistic striving may lead to addictive efforts to measure up to this god's expectations, and in the process we may abuse or abandon ourselves and others in our attempts to please a god who is impossible to please.

EXPERIENCING DISCOMFORT ABOUT OUR DISTORTED IMAGES OF GOD

When we finally recognize that our private images of God are destructive, we may feel horrified at the thought that we could entertain such negative images of God. In spite of our discomfort, it is critical that we explore our private images of God because of the power that these images have in our lives. If these fearful images of God and shaming beliefs about ourselves are the foundation on which we have built our spiritual lives, then we must expose our fears and shame so that we can begin reconstructing our spiritual lives on the secure foundation of grace. As long as we consciously or unconsciously cling to our idolatrous attachments that grow out of our fear and shame, we limit our ability to surrender to God's love. If the God of our experience is anything other than the God of love and grace, and our self-image is anything other than that we are dearly loved by God, it is time to start rebuilding our spiritual lives from the ground up. We need to demolish the house we have built on sand, and seek out some solid rock on which to rebuild.

ASSESSING THE DAMAGE

At this point, you might be experiencing some anxiety or confusion. Maybe some of the not-Gods we have described seem like accurate descriptions of God to you. Or maybe your beliefs about yourself as unlovable or without value seem like the truth. Perhaps the idea that you will need to get rid of all the not-Gods in your life terrifies you. Some of us reach this point and wonder if there will be any God left when we get rid of all the distortions. We fear that, once we tear down our damaged spiritual life, we will be forced to live forever in its ruins. We may fear that once we get rid of all the distortions and not-Gods, we will be left spiritually broken and alone. All of these concerns are understandable. We understand that assessing the damage caused by our fear and shame is difficult and painful, but we encourage you to stay with the process. It is only after taking this kind of hard look at our spiritual foundations that we can proceed toward rebuilding our spiritual lives on a more secure foundation. As we begin to see the not-Gods we have been serving, we will see also that we need to begin our spiritual rebuilding project by saying *no* to the gods-who-are-not-God. Any part of our spiritual life that is built on top of these poor substitutes will need to be torn down before serious reconstruction can begin.

If you are struggling to assess whether you worship a god who is not God, we propose a straightforward test:

1. Sit down with paper and pen, and try to clear your mind of distractions.

2. Write as many descriptive words as you can about how you picture God when you are alone or when you are anxious. Take as long as you need.

3. List any fears you have when you think about God. To create this list honestly, try to put all your formal beliefs aside for now and answer only from the perspective of your actual, lived experience. Take as long as you need.

4. Open your Bible to 1 Corinthians 13:4-7. This passage describes the living and true God, who is love and who loves us perfectly. Make a list of the phrases that describe love, and substitute the word *God* for the word *love* (or *charity*, depending on your translation). Your list will read "God is patient, God is kind" and so on.

5. Look at the lists you created in steps 2, 3 and 4, side by side. How do your lists compare to the step 4 list?

If our lived experience of God is that God is less than perfectly loving, our lists will be different from the description in the Scripture passage. The extent to which our experience of God deviates from the reality of God's love and grace is the extent to which it is critical that we tear down our existing structure, remove the foundation, and start rebuilding.

QUESTIONS FOR PERSONAL REFLECTION

1. Which of the distorted images of God described in this chapter do you recognize as part of your experience?

2. Take time to do the exercise described in the preceding section of this chapter. What do you observe about your personal images of God from this exercise?

3. Which qualities of the God-who-is-love might be the most helpful to you as you begin to rebuild a damaged spiritual life?

PART 2

TOOLS FOR RECONSTRUCTION

6

BEGINNING TO REBUILD

Unless the LORD builds the house,
its builders labor in vain.

PSALM 127:1

We are now ready to outline a blueprint for rebuilding our spiritual lives. By *blueprint* we mean a general plan for rebuilding; the specifics of the rebuilding process will vary significantly from person to person. The blueprint begins with the recognition that we need to tear up our old foundation and get to work on a new one—in other words, we focus first and foremost on rebuilding our relationship with God. So we begin by asking what kind of relationship we plan to build.

We are convinced that all of us long for a relationship with God—a relationship characterized by intimacy and loving respect. We are convinced that this longing is hard-wired into us. It is part of who we are. Perhaps these longings are buried and unconscious, but they are there. We do not want an abusive relationship with God, nor do we want a distant relationship with God. We long for the security, connectedness and closeness that can come only from an intimate relationship with God. Fortunately, even a casual reading of the Bible suggests that this is precisely the kind of relationship God wants to have with us. The problem is that those of us who are experiencing the kinds of destructive spirituality that is described in the previous chapters of this book must face the fact that our relationship with God is not an intimate one; it is not characterized by either closeness or respect. Many of us must begin the process of rebuilding our spiritual lives by recognizing that our relationship with God is best character- ized as either an actively or quietly abusive relationship, because we have been serving gods-who-are-not-God. These not-Gods have been abusive, neglectful, distant and shaming. If this is the case, the central question for us is this: how can we move from an abusive relation- ship with a god-who-is-not-God to an intimate relationship with the true and living God? That's what we want, and that's what the God revealed in Scripture wants as well.

To understand this blueprint for rebuilding our spiritual lives, we have found it helpful to look at a grid that illustrates some distinct types of relationships. We are indebted here to Merle A. Fossum and Mari- lyn J. Mason, whose book *Facing Shame: Families in Recovery* emphasizes two key qualities of relationships. First, all relationships—including our relationship with God—fall somewhere on a continuum between *hot* relationships and *cool* relationships (see fig. 1). By hot relationships we mean close, engaged, face-to-face relationships. By cool relation- ships we mean controlled, cautious, limited relationships. Second, all relationships fall somewhere on a continuum between respectful and shaming relationships. In respectful relationships, each party treats the other as a valued person, whereas in shaming relationships, one or both parties devalue the other in some way.

When we put these two qualities together, we can distinguish be- tween four distinct kinds of relationships.

Actively abusive relationships. A relationship that is hot and is char- acterized by shame is what we call an actively abusive relationship. If we were talking about domestic violence, this would be the kind

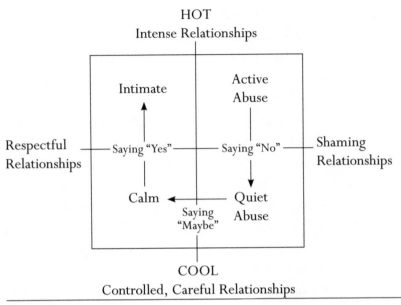

Figure 1.

of relationship likely to result in physical bruises and broken bones in addition to psychological and spiritual trauma. Both the intensity and the shame are very high.

Quietly abusive relationships. It is also possible to have a relationship that is shaming but cool. We call this a quietly abusive relationship. Taking domestic violence again as an example, a quietly abusive relationship would not involve bruises and broken bones, but it would still cause the kinds of damage that come from shame. The intensity is reduced—almost certainly a good thing in the case of violent relationships—but the level of shame is still very high.

Calm relationships. A relationship that is cool but is also high in respect is what we call a calm relationship. It may not be an intimate relationship, but because the shame is low and the respect is high, it can offer many benefits, such as safe companionship.

Intimate relationships. Intimate relationships are hot (close, deeply connected) and profoundly respectful, which is a powerful combination. All of us gravitate, when we feel it is safe to do so, in the direction of increased intimacy. We long to be deeply known, understood and loved. And we also long to know others deeply, to understand them and to love them. This is possible only in relationships that are both respectful and very close.

So how does our relationship with God fit into this pattern? Those of us who have found some elements of active abuse in our relationship with God long for that relationship to become both hot (close) and respectful. It would be great if we could just move directly, in a single step, from an actively abusive relationship to an intimate one. Since both kinds of relationships are hot, maybe it would work to just remove the shame in the relationship and replace it with respect. While such a transition might be possible in theory, all our experience suggests that there is no way to do this. Again using the analogy of domestic violence, a physically abused spouse often experiences times of deep longing for the return of intimacy—and may often attempt to make this one-step transformation. But the results are unfortunately predictable. The attempt to shift quickly to an intimate relationship turns out to be just another stage in the cycle of abuse. It may briefly seem that a transformation has taken place and intimacy has returned, but sooner or later the same old abusive dynamics take over.

After a few trips around this cycle, we learn that in our efforts to make a quick, one-step escape from abuse into intimacy we must have overlooked some important steps in the healing process. And that is exactly the problem. We can't move directly from an abusive relationship to an intimate one. The blueprint we are proposing in this chapter involves three essential stages in the journey from an abusive relationship to an intimate relationship. We call these stages (1) the No stage, which is when we tear out our old, flawed foundation, (2) the Maybe stage, when we start building a new foundation, and (3) the Yes stage, when our foundation in a new relationship with God begins to support the weight of a new spiritual life.

In the first stage we say no to the gods-who-are-not-God, so that we can remove our faulty foundation. If we serve a god-who-is-not-God, a god who does not deserve our worship and service, we need to fire this god. The No stage reduces the intensity of the relationship, and this can't be avoided, because things need to calm down. We have to stop the active abuse—the bruises, the broken bones—before we can move on. In the Maybe stage we begin to explore the possibility of a more respectful relationship with God. This stage allows to us to gradually decrease the shame we experience in our relationship with God and helps us begin to experience God's love for us. And, finally, after we've spent time building trust during the Maybe stage, we find ourselves ready to begin to say yes to a more intimate relationship with God.

We want to be clear that these stages are not a simple "three steps and you're done" solution. Life is more complex than that. Some of us will find ourselves moving back and forth between stages, or we might feel like we are cycling through them. The purpose of this blueprint is not to provide a simple cut-and-dry solution, but to map out some important features of the rebuilding process.

SAYING NO

Perhaps you have been taught that having a relationship with God begins by saying yes. We were taught that as well. But the Bible is clear about this: If we serve gods-who-are-not-God, we must begin the rebuilding process by saying no to those gods. Dale's experience with this stage of the rebuilding process demonstrates some of its important features.

There was a time when it became clear to me that the god I served was not God. I lived in relationship with a god who was quick to anger and slow to forgive. That's not, of course, what I believed to be true about God, but if you had taken a close look at my spiritual life at that time, you probably would have observed a huge disconnect between what I believed and the realities of my spiritual life. I served a god who was impossible to please.

Over time I grew weary of trying to be good enough, dedicated enough, strong enough, smart enough or whatever enough to please my impossible-to-please god, and I found myself saying no. I was no longer willing to do the same thing over and over again, expecting different results. What followed was a season of deep spiritual distress. I wanted the living and true God to rush right in to replace the impostor I had been serving. But what I experienced was God's silence. This silence was the most difficult part of that season in my life. God apparently had nothing to say. Not a peep.

Finally, I summoned the courage to share my struggles with some other Christians. While God still seemed to have nothing to say, his followers could not stop talking. Everyone had something to say, a verse to read or advice to give. "Have you prayed about it?" "All things work together for good." "If you don't feel close to God, guess who moved?" The advice was glib, dismissive and shaming. I put these people who spoke too soon and too glibly on a list of people not to be trusted again with my spiritual struggles.

Eventually, I realized that all my efforts to get closer to God were counterproductive, and I gave up trying to force the feeling of closeness. I waited for God to speak in God's own time, unsure if that time would ever come. I was still pretty sure I knew what God would say to me, if anything. God would surely browbeat me by saying something like, "Think of everything we could have gotten done while you wasted all this time! I've been here all along. Where have you been?" These were the messages I expected to receive. But if God had spoken too soon, too glibly or in such a shaming manner, I know what I would have done. I would have added God's name to the list of people who could not be trusted with my spiritual brokenness.

When God did eventually speak, what I heard was absolutely the last thing I had ever expected God to say. God said, "Blessed are the spiritually broken. Come and rest." I had shamed myself relentlessly for my spiritual brokenness. I was supposed to be stronger, to be better, to be more successful spiritually. And others had added to this shame. But God did not add to this shame. God saw in my "no"—in my spiritual brokenness—an opportunity for spiritual blessing. I could not see it at the time; I thought saying no was a kind of failure. But God could see what I could not see: that I would never be able to say yes until I had said no to the gods-who-are-not-God. In retrospect, I can see that the important thing was not whether God was silent or talkative. The important thing was that God's silence was a respectful silence. God was not glib or dismissive. God did not talk too soon. God's silence had been an expression of care and respect.

If we are serving gods-who-are-not-God, the first step in spiritual rebuilding is for us to say no to those gods. As long as our hearts are turned toward false gods, we are unable to let ourselves experience God's grace. Saying no can be a scary step to take. We may be firing the only God we have ever served. The result is likely to be a season of spiritual distress, a season perhaps of doubts, second thoughts, spiritual confusion and spiritual loneliness. After all, our false gods provide us with some benefits. They are familiar. They are what we know. And sometimes the familiar, even if it is abusive, seems less terrifying than the fears that come when we think about firing the only god we have ever known.

In all the spiritual distress that accompanies saying no, it is difficult for us to remember that God's feelings about our spiritual brokenness are not the same as our own. The God we find in the Bible is clear about spiritual brokenness:

> The sacrifices of God are a broken spirit;
>   a broken and contrite heart,
>   O God, you will not despise. (Psalm 51:17)

We tend to despise our spiritual brokenness. We hate it. But God sees it differently. Not only does God not despise our spiritual brokenness; God sees it as a kind of worship, as a kind of sacrifice. God understands how painful it is to say no to our idolatrous attachments. God understands how difficult it is to let go. But God also recognizes the spiritual maturity that is being shaped within us during this difficult process. Jesus made exactly this point when he said,

> Blessed are the poor in spirit,
>   for theirs is the kingdom of heaven. (Matthew 5:3)

Contrary to all our expectations about our spiritual impoverishment, God sees past our confusion, our doubt and our distress to the growing spiritual humility that is a sign of our participation in the kingdom of heaven.

SAYING MAYBE

Dale's spiritual reconstruction project began when he said no to the gods-who-are-not-God. The season of No was a time of deep spiritual distress, but it led to the next stage of the rebuilding process. This next stage is full of "maybes." Maybe God's silence isn't a sign of God's absence. Maybe the silence is a respectful silence. Maybe. But maybe not. In the brokenness and silence that we experience following our dismissal of gods-who-are-not-God the living and true God is making space in our hearts where the Spirit can live. It may feel at first like a terrible emptiness within us. The demolition of unstable foundations often feels like that. It feels like things are being torn down and what is to come is not yet clear. But demolition is a necessary step in the rebuilding process. Fortunately, it is not the end of the process but just a stage on the way.

All of us who have served gods-who-are-not-God have been spiritually bloodied and bruised. As a result, we are understandably guarded, cautious and afraid. But a longing for grace and love is awakened in us and begins to push us to seek conscious contact with the God who is love. We find ourselves hesitant. During this Maybe stage we may find ourselves painfully aware of the partial and tentative nature of our commitments. We want to give ourselves to God without reservation, but we are afraid and we hold back. Our maybe can't yet become an unqualified yes.

Most of us have been told, perhaps over and over again, that God does not tolerate faith that is combined with doubt. As a consequence we may experience a good deal of shame during the Maybe stage of the spiritual rebuilding process. Saying maybe is a kind of holding back—of protecting ourselves just in case things are not safe. It can be helpful during this stage to remind ourselves of Jesus' response to the man in the Gospel of Mark who cried, "I do believe; help me overcome my unbelief!" (Mark 9:24). Jesus did not reject this man's faith. He did not say, "Come back later when you are ready to be totally committed." He did not shame him for his mixture of belief and unbelief. Instead, Jesus welcomed this man's maybe-faith.

If we have been living with destructive spirituality for a long time, we probably spend a significant amount of time living a guarded spiritual life. The two most prominent features of a guarded spiritual life are hypervigilance and dissociation.

Hypervigilance is a kind of early warning system we develop to protect ourselves. It is a state of heightened alertness—of being on guard against danger. We have experienced spiritual damage before, and we don't want to get hurt again. So we are watchful, careful, guarded and hesitant. We turn our radar for spiritual danger up as high as it will go, and at the slightest indication of a threat, we react in full force. Unfortunately, we may find that we are perpetually on guard, even when the situation does not call for us to be in such a defensive posture.

Dissociation is also a kind of defensive strategy. It is a strategic withdrawal in which we unknowingly numb our minds or get lost in thoughts about something other than what is happening in the moment. If hypervigilance is like an early warning radar system, dissociation is like a bunker in which we protect part of ourselves from perceived danger or like keeping part of ourselves in reserve. We don't want everything to be vulnerable again—not yet, not until we know it is safe. Many of us who have suffered from destructive spirituality know what it is like to go to church, sit down and tune out. When the service is over, we can't remember what happened; it's like we weren't there. It makes sense for us to do this in shaming, abusive churches, but we may find ourselves using this same strategy in grace-filled churches as well.

It is important to emphasize that hypervigilance and dissociation are good and useful skills. They can save our lives in genuinely dangerous situations, like on a battlefield. Paying attention to threats and protecting ourselves against vulnerabilities are helpful things to do in dangerous situations. However, they are less useful when we are trying to build our relationship with a graceful and loving God. Rather than protecting us as they did in the past, these protective instincts may get in our way.

Of course, our goal in life is not to be inattentive and undefended. The question for us is whether we can develop a healthy alertness and healthy boundaries in our relationship with God. There is something important about not trusting God and spiritual things too quickly. If we are anxious about something or are having difficulty trusting, we can allow ourselves the freedom to test the waters. Is this situation really safe? Is God going to help me out in this area of my life? We do need to be on guard enough to make sure we are not replacing one form of destructive spirituality with another. We need to be alert about what we are gravitating toward, to make sure it brings us closer to grace.

Fortunately, God is kind and patient. God is a gentle and persistent healer. God will encourage us to move along at whatever pace we can handle. Our hearts may feel hard and defended during this part of the rebuilding process, but we are in the midst of a huge transformation. Ezekiel described God's role in the process this way: "I will remove from them their heart of stone and give them a heart of flesh" (Ezekiel 11:19). God understands and is prepared to work with people who have well-defended, bunkered-down, well-guarded stone hearts. God understands that stone hearts have an appeal; you can't hurt a stone heart. God understands that flesh hearts are riskier; they can be hurt. And God is willing to be actively involved with us in the process of learning to be safe again.

Whatever the destructive spiritual patterns are that we are struggling with, it will take humility and courage to say maybe to the God
of grace. But each step of humility and courage that we take will be
met by the God who, like the waiting father in Jesus' story, scans the
horizon, waiting for our return, and runs to greet us with an embrace
of love. With each step we take, we will begin to experience more and
more of the love and grace that are all around us. The more we experience of this love and grace, the more we will find that we are free to
consider saying a clear and grateful yes to God.

SAYING YES

As we gradually build a sense of safety and security in the Maybe stage
of the rebuilding process, we will find ourselves more and more able
to consider saying yes to God. Every interaction with God that we
experience as respectful rather than shaming will build our conviction that our defensive posture may not be as necessary as it was in
the past.

We may think that the Yes phase will be the fun part. And there's a
lot of truth to that. But there are some surprising challenges in the Yes
stage. First, we may not yet be very skilled at intimate relationships.
We have been alert and on guard for a long time, so relaxing enough
to enjoy intimacy with God may be difficult.

One image of this stage of the rebuilding process that we have found
to be helpful is that of the prodigal son when he is at the party given by
his father (Luke 15:11-32). It is common to think of the prodigal son
as struggling intensely when he is in the "distant country," aware that
he has blown his inheritance and that the pigs are eating better than
he is. But we tend to overlook the anxiety he experiences on the way
home, hoping desperately that his father will at least accept him as a
servant. Even more overlooked is the struggle that the prodigal son

surely experiences as he stands in the middle of the elaborate celebration his father has prepared. He must have felt awkward, unworthy and completely out of place. How should he behave? How should he receive this gift? In some ways it would be easier to be a servant. A servant takes a low profile, does his job and that's that. But the honored guest? How was he to behave as an honored guest? It is not difficult to imagine that the father's love and grace could overwhelm him at first. This too-good-to-be-true feeling is a common feature of the saying yes part of the spiritual rebuilding process. It is a reminder that just because we are saying yes doesn't mean that our growth process has come to an end. Growing in our capacity to receive the love and grace of God is a lifelong adventure.

A second potential struggle in the Yes stage comes from the fact that the last time we were in a hot spiritual relationship, things did not go well. As we are able to say yes to God's grace, our relationship with God is becoming closer and more intimate. That is a good thing. It is what we want and what God wants. But there may be things about this new relationship that remind us of old shame and fear. We may run into some "triggers"—events or circumstances that remind us of the times when we had an actively abusive relationship with gods-who-were-not-God. Triggers are not very predictable. They can seem to appear out of nowhere. Like the prodigal right in the middle of the party, we might get triggered by something and feel again that compulsive need to be a servant rather than be the honored guest. Events like this are setbacks, sometimes taking us back to the Maybe stage. Sometimes they sweep us emotionally all the way back to the No stage, or at least that is how it feels. But every time it happens, we grow in our capacity to see it for what it is: a setback but not a complete collapse of the building.

A third dynamic that is often part of the Yes stage is that we find ourselves changing in our understanding of how God was involved in the earlier parts of our rebuilding process. During the No and Maybe stages of the rebuilding process, we may have looked forward to the Yes stage as a time when we would finally be able to enjoy being close to God. When we actually get to this stage, however, the situation seems more complex. We may begin to get a sense that God was close to us during the times that we were saying no—that God was supporting us and encouraging us even when we may not have wanted anything to do with God. When God was silent, we may have thought that God was distant and disinterested. But now we begin to see that God may have been just as close and attentive during those difficult times as we experience God to be now. Even as we were walking through the valley of the shadow of spiritual death, God was with us, guiding, supporting, leading and comforting us. Similarly, in the Maybe stage we may have thought that closeness to God would have to wait until all our questions and doubts and hesitations and fears were resolved. Now we may look back on that time and see that God was not impatiently waiting for us to resolve those things inside us. God was close all along. Close and pursuing. Close and persistent. Close and loving. In the midst of all our hesitation and defensiveness, God was on our side. God was working within us to calm our fears. While we were still broken, damaged, struggling and hesitant in faith, God was reaching out to us in love.

This sense that God has been with us all along and has been actively involved in our healing journey can be confusing at first. We may ask ourselves, *Why didn't I see this before?* But more important, this discovery can also be a powerful reminder that God has been saying yes to *us* all along. And as we are able to take in that remarkable fact, we may find that we are empowered to give voice to a yes of our own.

It can be helpful during the Yes stage to nurture an attitude of openness to surprise, to play and to rest. The Bible is full of stories about God working in surprising ways. God's surprises are never scare tactics; they are always gifts. God gives us exactly what we need, but God's gifts sometimes arrive in ways that surprise us. Sometimes this is God's way of inviting us to play. Play means we must relax our hypervigilance and crawl out of our dissociative bunkers in order to fully participate in whatever God has planned. Those of us who have suffered a long time with destructive spirituality tend to take ourselves seriously, and this can make it difficult for us to say a full-throated, down-deep yes to God.

If surprise or play seems too ambitious to you at this point in your recovery journey, perhaps focusing on rest will get you started. Rest is a central theme in the biblical text. God created and then rested. Rest is presented in Scripture as a nonnegotiable part of the spiritual life. Try to imagine a rest so comprehensive, so deep, so unrestrained that it could be called rest for your soul (Matthew 11:29). Learning to say yes to that kind of rest can be the beginning of many other kinds of yes in our relationship with God.

It may also be helpful in this stage to remind ourselves that God rejoices over us. The prodigal's father is only one of many biblical images of God as the one who throws a party for us. Consider what the prophet Zephaniah says:

> The LORD your God is with you,
>   he is mighty to save.
> He will take great delight in you,
>   he will quiet you with his love,
>   he will rejoice over you with singing. (Zephaniah 3:17)

God insists on celebrating with us even if we are still anxious and uncomfortable at the party. Over time, God's persistent love will quiet us, and in the quiet we may hear a remarkable sound: God singing. The song is a happy one. Allow God's love to quiet your heart. Allow yourself to respond with a yes to God's invitation to the party.

QUESTIONS FOR PERSONAL REFLECTION

1. What is difficult for you about saying no to gods-who-are-not-God?

2. What might it be like for you to say no to those gods? How difficult is it for you to imagine that the spiritual brokenness of saying no might be an opportunity for God to bless you?

3. What experiences have you had in saying maybe to God? What about this was difficult for you?

4. How might Jesus' acceptance of the man who said, "I do believe; help me overcome my unbelief!" help to you to be less judgmental toward yourself when you are saying maybe to God?

5. What experiences have you had in saying yes to God?

6. Read Zephaniah 3:17 as if God were saying yes directly to you. Write about your response to this text.

7
BUILDING A SOLID
SPIRITUAL FRAMEWORK

There are people who try to raise their souls like a man continually
taking standing jumps in the hopes that, if he jumps higher every day,
a time may come when he will no longer fall back but will go right up
to the sky. Thus occupied he cannot look at the sky. We cannot take a
single step toward heaven. It is not in our power to travel in a vertical
direction. If however we look heavenward for a long time, God comes
and takes us up. God raises us easily.

SIMONE WEIL

If any of us happened to see some people laying new carpet in a home
infested with termites, or putting up new wallpaper in a house that is
slowly caving in, we would call those people misguided. They don't
have their priorities straight, we would say. You have to have a solid
structure before you worry about carpet and wallpaper. However,
when it comes to addressing the damage in our spiritual structures,
most of us behave in ways that are just as unproductive. We try to
repair or redecorate rather than make a full assessment of the damage and commit ourselves to whatever demolition and rebuilding is
required.

If we have experienced the kind of destructive spirituality described in this book, putting up a new Bible verse on the wall is not going to get done what we need to get done.

The people who are laying carpet over their termite infestation would have benefited from a visit with a building contractor or exterminator—someone who has experience in assessing and repairing homes. Likewise, when rebuilding a damaged spiritual life, one of the first things we need to do is to be sure that we have strong structures in place to support the process.

But what makes for a solid spiritual structure? What's helpful? Unfortunately, many of the things we tend to try first when we are feeling like spiritual failures or feeling like we are spiritually damaged do not help at all. In this chapter we will look at some of these unhelpful strategies and try to find some more productive alternatives. You may recognize yourself more than once as we look at strategies that are not helpful. All of us have tried these strategies at one time or another. Some of us have tried all of these strategies, sometimes repeatedly. The purpose of taking a close look at what doesn't help is not to make us feel bad about the amount of time and energy that we have spent in counterproductive rebuilding efforts. Rather, this chapter is intended to give us an opportunity to reevaluate our ineffective behaviors and to look for something that is actually helpful in the process of rebuilding our spiritual lives.

FROM DENIAL TO EMBRACING THE TRUTH

When we look at our spiritual lives and find that we are caught up in destructive spirituality, we are often tempted to tell ourselves that the problems we have identified are not real or that we are exaggerating their importance. There are lots of ways we try to avoid the truth about our spiritual brokenness. A spiritually addicted pastor might say, "I'm not a ministry addict. I just I love my work." A person who is spiritually codependent may insist that "I'm just trying to be helpful." Someone who is spiritually anorexic might say, "God expects us to be a living sacrifice, and that means doing without." And a person engaged in abusive spirituality might say, "I'm not being abusive. It's part of our calling to identify moral evil and to confront it when we find it." Statements like these are ways of minimizing and denying the destructive nature of our damaged spirituality.

Denial is not always this obvious and direct. Any strategy that minimizes or avoids the reality of our destructive spiritual patterns is part of the problem, not part of the solution. The reason why denial has such an appeal is that staying aware of our spiritual brokenness and the harm it does to us and to others is personally painful. It is a challenge to face the truth about our spiritual condition and to stay conscious of that reality. But we can't address a problem and pretend it doesn't exist at the same time. In order to begin the healing process, we need to accept our condition and continue to confront ourselves with that truth so that we can remain aware enough to address what is wrong. If we can identify with one or more of the kinds of spiritual brokenness that we talked about earlier, it is a problem, and the problem is serious enough to require us to take some action.

FROM QUICK FIXES TO LETTING IT TAKE AS LONG AS IT TAKES

Most of us who recognize the need to rebuild our spiritual lives wish we could make our problems rapidly disappear. Dale remembers a time early in his own recovery when he prayed, "I don't care how painful the solution is, God, if only it can be fixed quickly." This is a very common longing when we begin to rebuild a damaged spiritual life, and many of us have tried every quick fix we could think of before getting down to the work of rebuilding.

Some of us rededicated our lives to Christ and really meant it every time. Others of us found a new church or found a new Bible study group that we thought would provide us with the answers. Many of us tried getting up earlier in the morning and praying longer and harder than ever before, in the hope that this extra effort would fix our problems. Some of us tried leaving our problems at the foot of the cross. Many of us read books (like this one), hoping that by the time we had finished reading, our lives would be changed. Others have found "heroes of the faith" to emulate.

All of these get-it-over-with-quickly strategies have an understandable appeal. Speed is a high value in our culture. Faster computers are better computers. Faster cars are better cars. Fast is good, slow is bad, so we try to keep going fast. We are also attracted to spiritual things that happen quickly—like miracles and instantaneous healings. We want our spiritual lives to be like Paul's experience on the road to Damascus—quick, decisive and miraculous. But the God of the Bible does not appear to be as enamored with speed as we are.

God knows that some things take time. God is patient. And even though it may not be what we would prefer, God's patience is good news, because things that are done quickly are sometimes not done thoroughly.

Imagine that after having surgery to remove a cancerous tumor the doctor comes to see you. Your first question probably won't be, How long did it take? The important question is, Did you get it all? Thoroughness is an essential element both in surgery and in the process of rebuilding a damaged spiritual life. We don't want to slap a quick coat of paint on the unstable house to make it look better. We want, instead, to identify everything that needs attention, and then do a thorough, comprehensive repair. That takes time.

FROM SHAMING OURSELVES TO SEEING OURSELVES AS GOD SEES US

People who struggle with the kinds of spiritual damage that we are talking about in this book almost always struggle with shame. Shame is not the same as guilt. Guilt is the emotional response we have when we feel we have done something wrong. Shame, however, is an abiding belief or mindset that we are unlovable or without value. Guilt, as many have noted, is about what I have done; shame is about who I am. When we feel shame, we collapse in upon ourselves emotionally, afraid that we just don't measure up and that we never will. Shame paralyzes us and leaves us in a place of despair. Shame is profoundly damaging to our spiritual lives, and yet it is common for us to think that the solution to our problems might be to increase our shame rather than to decrease it.

In response to your struggles, you may have heard, "If you just trusted God enough, it wouldn't be a problem." This statement can be an invitation to shame. It suggests that we should be ashamed of ourselves for not being spiritually healthy. This kind of judgment can have an enormous appeal. The hope—however bizarre it may seem when we say it clearly—is that maybe if we just feel bad enough, maybe if we increase our shame enough, maybe if we get depressed enough about our failures, somehow things will change for the better in our relationship with God.

But shame can never provide a suitable foundation for a healthy spiritual life. It just doesn't work. In any other relationship this is perfectly obvious. Suppose someone who is struggling in a troubled marriage said to you, "I'm going to fix this relationship by reminding myself every day that I am worthless and unlovable." This would, of course, be a symptom of the problem, not part of the solution. The same is true in our relationship with God. Shaming ourselves for our spiritual brokenness is not the solution. What we need is not more shame, but to be healed of our shame. In order to rebuild our lives on the solid foundation of God's love, we need God to give us new eyes to see ourselves without the distortion of shame.

From Trying Harder to Relying on Grace

When our spiritual lives are badly damaged, we may want to fix the problem by trying harder. If reading the Bible and praying are our central spiritual disciplines and they're not working, we may decide to read the Bible more and to pray more—more often and with more intensity. When that doesn't work, we may want to try even harder, and then we try our hardest. And then what? Usually, we get tired, discouraged, angry and resentful. We might say, "This is supposed to be working. Why does it seem like I'm just digging myself into a deeper hole?"

When addressing spiritual issues, trying harder is rarely, if ever, part of the solution. In fact, trying harder is part of the problem. One popular definition of insanity is "doing the same thing over and over again and expecting different results." When our spiritual lives are badly damaged, it isn't reasonable to expect the solution to be as simple as doing the same stuff we have been doing but doing it with more intensity, or more sincerity or more frequency. What happens is that we get trapped in a performance-oriented spirituality. We have to work harder and harder to maintain the illusion that we have this problem under control. Eventually, nothing we do helps.

Our situation is similar to that of an alcoholic who tries to stay sober by sheer force of will—by trying really hard not to drink. This strategy is often called white-knuckle sobriety, as if the alcoholic were hanging on to sobriety tightly enough to force all the blood from his or her fists. And we call this person a dry drunk—depressed, cynical, critical, but not drinking right now. It takes an enormous amount of effort for the alcoholic to will him- or herself into not drinking, and these efforts usually fail.

It takes an equally enormous amount of effort when a spiritually wounded person attempts to will him- or herself into a healthier spiritual life. White-knuckle spirituality does not work any more than white-knuckle sobriety. Sooner or later the effort required exhausts us to the point that we can no longer keep it up. The result of trying harder is that we become depressed, irritable and cynical, and eventually we give up completely. We become a dry believer. If we want to do some serious rebuilding of our damaged spiritual lives, sooner or later we will need to stop trying to do the work ourselves and to learn ways of actively relying on the grace of God. In practical terms this means that we need to put into practice the first three steps of any Twelve Step program. First, we acknowledge that we are powerless over our spiritual brokenness and that our lives have become unmanageable. Second, we acknowledge that there is a Power greater than ourselves who can restore us. And finally, we make a daily decision to turn our lives and wills over to God's loving care so that God can heal our spiritual wounds.

FROM BLAMING OTHERS TO OWNING OUR LIVES

When we begin the process of rebuilding a damaged spiritual life, we may find ourselves looking around at smoldering ruins and asking a lot of questions. How did this happen? Who did this? Who is responsible for this mess? Even a little reflection will suggest that the answers to these questions are not simple. We can probably identify people who contributed to the mess. Our spiritual damage often has a long family history. Religious addicts, for example, frequently find that the addictive process is evident in a variety of ways in their family systems, often over many generations. It rarely emerges out of nowhere. The same is true of other kinds of distorted spiritualities; they have a history. As this reality becomes clear to us, it is easy for us to get distracted by blame.

Let's face it: blame is attractive at first. It can be a relief to find the "bad guys" and to spend time and energy focused on their problems and their failures. But blame does not lead us to where we want to go. It leads most frequently to resentments, and resentments are a kind of toxin that can undermine all our efforts at spiritual growth. We need to do whatever it takes to avoid getting stuck in blame and to focus on our own issues—not because we are responsible for everything that has gone wrong but because the only problems that we can productively work on are our own problems. The process of rebuilding a damaged spiritual life does not begin until I start to face my issues, my struggles and my brokenness. As long as I am focused on the problems of others, I am at risk of being distracted. It's not a matter of switching blame from others to ourselves; it's about investing productively in change that can really make a difference in our lives.

FROM DESPAIR TO STAYING OPEN TO HOPE

After we have tried several unhelpful strategies for fixing our spiritual brokenness, we are tempted to fall into despair. Despair can be a defense, because we can numb ourselves with it, telling ourselves it is futile to care anymore. Although despair is painful, we can hide behind it, hoping it will be less painful than staying with the painful reality of our spiritual brokenness. Some of us hide behind our despair for a long time. It hurts to hope that there is love and goodness in the world when we have not experienced much of it.

Grace awakens the deepest longing within us—a longing to love and be loved, whereas despair protects us from the risks of hope and the pain of this longing. Despair also effectively closes us off from the experience of grace. When our strategies for dealing with our spiritual brokenness fail us, we can feel like there is no hope left for us. Ironically, this kind of breakdown is actually the beginning of true hope. It's when we come to the terrifying end of our own resources that it becomes possible to see the beginnings of grace. It is painful to allow ourselves to hope that God can and will do what we cannot do, but the smallest flicker of such hope—the smallest mustard seed of such faith—opens the way for God's transforming love to move mountains.

FROM ISOLATION TO SEEKING HELP AND SUPPORT

One of the first strategies we adopt when we recognize the extent of the spiritual damage in our lives is isolation. There are good reasons for this instinct. First, we isolate ourselves because we are afraid. We know we are capable of hurting other people, and so we seek the apparent safety of isolation. Second, we isolate ourselves because we know that other people can hurt us. We have been hurt in relationships before, and the last thing we need right now is to share our spiritual brokenness with someone who might be glib or dismissive. We don't need any more shame. We don't need any more rejection. So we decide to isolate ourselves.

But we need, and have always needed, other people. We are not remotely close to being self-sufficient. It is possible to sustain the pretense for a while, but at some point the effort required to sustain the illusion of self-sufficiency becomes too great, and we wind up exhausted, frustrated and depressed. The realities of life force us, eventually, to face the fact that we cannot survive in isolation. We need a safe community in which to heal.

CONCLUSION

Rebuilding a damaged spiritual life begins with taking a close look at how committed we are to denial, quick fixes, shame, blame, trying harder, despair and isolation. These strategies are all part of the spiritually destructive patterns that have entangled us. Making an assessment of how much energy we are spending on these and other similarly unhelpful strategies is an important step in the rebuilding process. It will be necessary for us to let go of strategies that do not work and to replace them with strategies that help us to embrace truth, tolerate patience, receive grace, increase our dependence on God, take responsibility, sustain hope and lead us to accept help. In coming chapters we will look at some practical ways to actually make progress on some of these more helpful strategies.

QUESTIONS FOR PERSONAL REFLECTION

1. This chapter discusses seven common mistakes people make when rebuilding a damaged spiritual life: denial, quick fixes, shame, trying harder, blame, despair and isolation. What personal experience do you have with these strategies?

2. What problems have these strategies created in your life?

3. The chapter also suggests seven helpful ways to approach spiritual change: embracing the truth, letting the process take time, letting go of shame, letting go of trying harder, taking ownership of the problem, staying open to hope and asking for help. What has been your personal experience of these strategies?

4. Which of these issues do you think needs to be your primary focus right now?

8

RELYING ON GOD

The prayer of the heart challenges us to hide absolutely nothing from God and to surrender ourselves unconditionally to his mercy. Thus the prayer of the heart is the prayer of truth.

HENRI NOUWEN

The rebuilding of a damaged spiritual life will be more efficient if we have the right tools. The tools we have found to be the most useful are some of the basic tools for spiritual growth found in the Christian tradition. There are certainly other tools that might be of use in the rebuilding process, but this chapter and those that follow are about the spiritual disciplines that we have found to be most helpful. The fact that these tools are spiritual disciplines with a long history may be a problem for some of us. Perhaps these tools are associated in our minds with the kinds of spiritual damage we have experienced. Some of us, for example, are Bible-phobic. If Scripture has been misused by us or by those with authority in our faith communities, we may find ourselves resistant to having anything to do with the Bible. Similarly, some of us may know only one way to pray, and that kind of prayer may be so associated with destructive spirituality that we lack any access to this means of communication with God. One of the most difficult aspects of destructive spirituality is the way it distorts the tools of vital Christian faith. Reclaiming these tools, however, can provide us with significant resources as we seek to rebuild our spiritual lives.

Fortunately, the Christian faith has a rich and diverse tradition. Many authors have written extensively about a wide range of spiritual practices that can open our lives more deeply to the experience of God's grace. What we hope to offer in these final chapters is a brief introduction to several spiritual tools, with a focus on how they might be useful to someone who is rebuilding a damaged spiritual life. As you will see, each tool has some potential for abuse; all of us are capable of misusing these tools. For example, some spiritual addicts may see in these tools a variety of ways to alter their mood. Some spiritual abusers may see a list of things they can use to show others how they are failing to measure up to God's expectations. Some spiritual codependents may see a list of things they are obligated to do—and make others do. And some spiritual anorexics may read these chapters and feel incapable of finding spiritual nurture from any of these practices. Each of us has our own way of distorting the tools of faith. However, these tools can also be powerful and positive forces in our lives. They can set in motion a new openness in our lives to direct experiences of God's love and grace.

As we describe each tool, we will point out some of its unique dangers and opportunities. A few words of advice: Don't try to put the whole list into practice at once. Start where you feel you need to start, or can start, and take your time. This list is not exhaustive, nor is it in-depth enough to explain everything there is to know about each tool. Our intention here is to provide a beginning—a portal into active faith for people who are beginning to rebuild a damaged spiritual life. We hope to help reclaim each of these tools from the distortions of destructive spirituality, explain the spirit and function of each tool, and suggest a first step toward putting each tool to practical use. We pray for God's blessing on you as you begin to apply one or more of these tools to the work of rebuilding your spiritual life.

The first tools we describe can be helpful in coming to the end of our self-reliance and finding practical ways to rely instead on the love and grace of God. The necessary starting point for learning how to use these tools is the recognition that we are not capable of rebuilding our spiritual lives by our own power alone. We can't be good enough, dedicated enough, sincere enough or anything enough to restore our spiritual lives to a healthy state. We need help. Surrendering and listening to God are two tools that help us let go of our own efforts and open our hearts to receive God's help and blessing.

SURRENDERING

Surrendering is about coming to the end of our own resources. David Benner, in his book *Surrender to Love*, describes surrender this way:

> The English word *surrender* carries the implication of putting one's full weight on someone or something. It involves letting go—a release of effort, tension and fear. And it involves trust. One cannot let go of self-dependence and transfer dependence to someone else without trust.
>
> Floating is a good illustration of this, because you cannot float until you let go. Floating is putting your full weight on the water and trusting that you will be supported. It is letting go of your natural instincts to fight against sinking. Only then do you discover that you are supported.

Although *surrender* is a word commonly used in a military context, spiritual surrender is not about losing or about being defeated. When we surrender spiritually, we gain enormously. The apostle Paul talked about his personal need for surrender in this way: "I do not understand what I do. For what I want to do I do not do, but what I hate I do. . . . What a wretched man I am! Who will rescue me from this body of death? Thanks be to God—through Jesus Christ our Lord!" (Romans 7:15, 24). In this text Paul speaks with great transparency about his experience of coming to the end of trying harder to be the person he thought God wanted him to be. It is at this point that Paul calls out for help and remembers with gratitude that help is available. When we come to the end of ourselves and finally see our need for God's help and grace, and have a glimmer of hope that God's grace might be available to us, we are ready to surrender.

Under the influence of destructive spirituality surrender can become distorted into one of two forms: resignation or compliance. Resignation means ceasing to resist the advances of a dominant other, and it feels something like this: *I can't win. I give up. Please don't hurt me.* Resignation in our relationship with God could suggest that we experience God as a bully who has finally beaten us down. The other distortion, compliance, is an act of self-will. Compliance feels something like this: *I don't really have any other choice, so I will force myself to adhere to the rules.* In some situations, compliance is appropriate. For example, we may appropriately make a conscious decision and exert personal effort to obey traffic laws. But to obey God's law in this way is to treat God as a traffic cop: if we try really hard, maybe God won't give us a ticket. Neither resignation nor compliance leads us to a healthier spiritual life.

Surrender is not like resignation because surrender means ceasing to resist the advances of a God who loves us and pursues us with grace. When we surrender, we let God's grace into our lives. We ask God to take over and to guide us. We give up the idea that we can run our lives effectively on our own. Surrender is not like compliance, either, because surrender is not an act of self-will. When we surrender, we give up our own efforts to make ourselves acceptable. We give up on the whole exhausting "try, try harder, try our hardest" pathway to spiritual growth.

In chapter four, we told the story of Alice, who suffered from spiritual codependency. Alice experienced anxiety about her siblings' spiritual lives and worked hard to control her family's relationship with God. Part of Alice's recovery was a kind of surrender to God's purposes. Instead of praying for God to change her siblings, Alice sat in silence and asked for eyes to see where God was working in her own life. In time, this led Alice to trust that God was working in the world. God was not a passive onlooker but was active in her life and in the lives of others. This new faith gave Alice the peace of mind she needed in order to surrender her attempts to control others.

Juanita's and Dale's understanding of surrender was profoundly affected the year that their oldest son dropped out of high school and became a drug addict. Here's how they talk about the experience:

It was a very dark and difficult year for us. It was also a time of deeper exposure to the dynamics of surrender. When our son was using, we thought we should be able to do all kinds of things that we could not do. Intellectually we knew better. Even experientially we knew better. But this was our child. Everything in us seemed to scream, *We should!* We should be able to figure out when he was using and when he was not. We should be able to reason with him. We should be able to make him stop. We should be able to keep him away from his using friends. We should be able to get him the right help. We should be able to protect him from harm, including his self-harm.

We tried. For months we tried. But we could not do any of those things. Believing we should be able to do what we could not do, and endlessly trying to control what we could not control, left us in our own insanity. It was only when we grew sick and tired of our own insanity that we were able to recognize that our lives had become unmanageable. And it was only then that we were ready to learn new lessons in humility.

Surrender helped to restore our sanity. We could not do for our son any of what we, as his parents, wanted so desperately to do. We could not. That simple truth was excruciatingly painful, and yet it was wonderfully freeing. And it ultimately was what opened the door for our healing as parents and for our healing as a family, because healing could occur only as we lived in that humble truth and got out of God's way. We stopped trying to do what only God could do when we humbly admitted, "We cannot."

The events with our son were of crisis proportions. And they helped us see our need for surrender in a big way. But surrender is also about the ordinary realities of everyday life. Whenever we observe ourselves growing anxious or angry or resentful, it is often a sign that we are trying to control something that is out of our control. It is a sign that we are trying to play God in our own lives or in the lives of others. Our anxiety, anger and resentments are often reminders to us to call on God's grace and guidance. They are reminders to surrender.

We can apply the tool of surrender to any situation in which we feel anxious or we want to control things that are not in our control—in our relationships, career, education, social life or parenting. Life is full of situations in which grace-filled surrender is a practical and helpful path. Surrender is a tool we can use every day, even every hour. We are more likely to experience peace when we can say, "Okay, God, I don't know what to do, and I'm asking for the knowledge of your will and the strength to follow the guidance you give me."

To truly surrender we must come to the end of our attempts to run our own lives. Once we are clear on the futility of our own spiritual efforts and the need for God's help and guidance, we can turn our lives over to God's care and direction. As long as some part of us is holding out and believing that we can make our lives work if we just try a little harder, we will find it difficult to fully surrender. Thus, surrendering to God's love and grace becomes a process of releasing more and more of our self-reliance as we grow in faith.

Equally important to effective surrender is the willingness to believe that God will take over when we come to the end of our futile attempts to be good enough, spiritual enough or smart enough to run our own lives. For most of us this is not an easy step to take. We may have had many experiences that led us to believe that God is not safe, and so surrendering to God may feel like a big risk. What if God abandons us? What if God has given up on us? When we surrender, it feels like we are gambling on the possibility that God's love is real. If we are willing to take this risk, the payoff will be a direct experience of God's grace at work in our lives.

As a first step toward the practice of surrender, it can be helpful to list the situations and people we are feeling anxious or angry about. We can then offer this list to God. We might want to start a "surrender box," where we leave this list and future lists. We might want to share our list with a trusted friend or spiritual partner. We might want to hold the list tightly in our hands as a symbol of our resistance to surrender, and then open our hands as a symbol of surrendering our fears, resentments and desires into God's control.

LISTENING TO GOD

Who we listen to while rebuilding a damaged spiritual life makes a lot of difference. Sometimes all kinds of people are talking to us. We may hear critical voices, annoying voices, helpful voices, fearful voices, shaming voices and hopeful voices. And to make matters worse, we likely are hearing a variety of inner voices as well. Most of us have an inner chorus that is quite capable of keeping the noise level up when the voices of real people fade away. Our inner chorus is often made up of powerful voices from our past—the voices of certain people that still influence us even though they are no longer part of our day-to-day lives. With all these voices competing for our attention, it is essential to develop spiritual practices that help our spirits listen to the loving voice of God.

Prayer, meditation and Scripture are three means of listening to God. These three spiritual practices have a long, rich history in the Christian tradition. Many books have been written about each of these practices and all the ways they can enrich our lives. Our focus here will be on using these practices as ways of tuning the ears of our spirits to listen to God as part of our daily reliance on God's healing, help and guidance.

When we pray, we talk to God and we listen to God. Prayer, therefore, is not only a means of relating directly to God; it is also a way of knowing ourselves to be in God's presence. Prayer begins with an honest acknowledgment of our need for God. Over and over again in Scripture we are invited to call for help whenever we need it because God is eager to respond to us. The book of Hebrews offers a helpful summary of what we can expect when we pray: "Let us then approach the throne of grace with confidence, so that we may receive mercy and find grace to help us in our time of need" (Hebrews 4:16).

In the context of dysfunctional spirituality, prayer can become easily distorted. Sometimes prayer becomes a list-making activity in which we expect God to respond to our priorities. We actively reverse roles with God by taking on the job of developing a to-do list and giving God the job of implementing our priorities. This kind of prayer will not help us in the spiritual rebuilding process, because it means we are still in charge. In this kind of prayer we miss the gifts that prayer offers. We miss the mercy. We miss the grace. We miss the loving voice of God.

Prayer can also become a rote exercise, just something we're supposed to do. It can be one of the many ways we perform to win God's approval. When it becomes disconnected from honesty and humility, it can easily become a formality—even an unwanted obligation. But prayer is not intended to be just part of our routine; it is designed to help us seek conscious contact with the true and living God. It is intended to remind us that we live in the presence of a God who seeks to bless, heal and help us.

To prepare ourselves to listen for God's voice, a good first step in prayer might be to follow the pattern of the psalmists, who often begin with an honest outpouring of their heart to God. In Psalm 62:8 we read:

> Trust in him at all times, O people;
>> pour out your hearts to him,
>> for God is our refuge.

Prayer is an invitation to share deeply and honestly all our thoughts, feelings, longings and needs with God. Often before we can listen, we need to talk—not telling God what to do, not trying to say things just right in a prayer of performance, but like a trusting child running to a safe and loving parent for comfort, help, guidance, support, forgiveness and love. It is often when we have poured out our hearts that we are ready to be quiet. The honest, trusting, childlike pouring out of our hearts opens our hearts, making us ready to listen to God and to receive from God.

A second practice that can help us listen to God is meditation. You might recall a verse that we discussed earlier in this book—"Be still, and know that I am God" (Psalm 46:10).

This is an invitation to meditate—in other words, to pray as an act of being still before God and opening ourselves to whatever God might show us. When we pour out our hearts to God, we prepare ourselves to receive from God and we open our hearts and minds to listen to God.

Just as there are dysfunctional ways to pray, there are also dysfunctional ways to meditate. For example, some people expect meditation to instantly transform their lives. But there is nothing magical about meditation. It is not a quick and easy, guaranteed way to change one's life. Nor is meditation very helpful if it reinforces a kind of mindlessness or dissociation that makes it harder to pay attention to what is real in our lives.

Meditation is the practice of listening carefully, thoughtfully and receptively to the truth about who God is. So when we meditate on God's unfailing love, for example, we allow the truth of God's love to sink deep within us—past our fears and defenses. We listen in stillness and quiet to this truth, and we continue to listen over a period of time, letting this truth find a home within us.

It might help us to think of meditation as the part of conversational prayer that happens when we are not talking. It is the part where we listen. It is good to ask for things in prayer, to pour out our hearts to God in prayer, to seek guidance from God in prayer. And then, after the asking, the pouring out and the seeking, we are invited to be quiet, to listen, to await God's response. Meditation is, in part, learning how to protect the silences in prayer. Any silence will be threatened by the many competing, internal voices who want to have their say. Meditation is the practice of being still and quieting ourselves so that God is allowed to speak.

A first step in meditation might be to focus for a few minutes on a phrase, like the phrase God's "unfailing love" in Psalm 48:9. If you'd like to try it right now, take a few slow, easy breaths to still yourself and simply repeat the phrase several times quietly. As other thoughts come, let them pass and come back to the words "God's unfailing love." Allow yourself to hear these words; allow them to speak to you. Then, for a time, be quiet and invite God to say to you whatever God desires to say. You may sense only silence. You may have a thought come to you. You may sense the still, quiet voice of God speaking to your spirit. Continue to listen throughout the day to the words "God's unfailing love" and to anything you sense God might be saying to you.

One of the difficulties of meditation is that when we listen to God, we may not like what God has to say. In the chapter on spiritual addiction (chap. 3), we told the story of Eric, who compulsively prayed and read the Bible as part of his addiction. Learning a meditative approach to both prayer and Scripture was critically important to his spiritual rebuilding process. Bob, the friend from Alcoholics Anonymous who met with Eric, suggested to Eric that instead of handing God a to-do list every morning, he might sit quietly and listen to see if God has anything to say. Eric stopped working so hard to perform for God in prayer; instead he began to sit in silence, listening for any hints of God's will for him. As Eric listened to God, he felt for the first time the pain that his actions had caused his wife and children. It was not easy to listen, and he heard many voices of shame, blame and accusation that competed for his attention. But as Eric learned to stay with the listening part of prayer, he was gradually able to stay focused on God's clear but painful message and not get lost in the babble of other voices. As a result, Eric was able to change his behavior and make appropriate amends to his wife and children. These changes brought grace and healing to Eric and his family. Over time he started to see the link between meditation and growth in his capacity to trust that, as Jesus promised, when he asks for bread, God won't give him a stone (Matthew 7:9, 11).

In addition to listening to God in prayer and in meditation, part of listening to God is to listen to the voice of Scripture. Relying on Scripture for guidance and wisdom can provide us with a practical safeguard against the many confusing voices that demand to be heard. As we listen to the text of Scripture, we find ourselves listening to a voice other than our own—a voice that is, thankfully, far more grace-filled and loving than many of the other voices that we could be paying attention to.

Like the other tools we have talked about in this chapter, the practice of reading and meditating on biblical texts can also become distorted. When we read the Bible, we bring to it whatever is going on inside us. If we suffer from destructive spirituality, we bring our inclinations to addiction, abuse, codependency and anorexia with us to the text. If we are serving gods-who-are-not-God, we bring our idolatrous attachments with us when we read Scripture. When this is the case, we read the Bible through a filter of fear, shame and self-reliance that effectively screens out the good news of God's active love for us. For example, we could read, "All things work together for good" (Romans 8:28 KJV) as if it were an injunction against grief. We might hear in our minds something dismissive or shaming, such as, *There is no reason to be sad, because this is a good thing. Get over it.* But this is not what the apostle Paul is saying. He is affirming that no matter what our circumstances, God is at work. If it is a time to grieve, then God grieves with us and is working in that grief—no matter how long it takes—to comfort us and to help us.

Another example of the way we might misread Scripture is in Philippians 3:13, where Paul says, "Forgetting what is behind, . . . I press on." When we read this text through the filter of shame, Paul may seem to be telling us to pay no attention to what has happened to us in the past—as if inattentiveness or having a poor memory were next to godliness! But that is the opposite of what Paul is saying. What Paul wants to leave behind is his life as a Pharisee—a life whose spirituality was based on fear, shame and performance. Paul is leaving behind his old, destructive spirituality, and he's pressing on to build a new life on grace. In Paul's past he was way too holy to grieve, way too spiritually advanced to struggle in life, and it is that denial system that he is trying to put behind him. He wants instead a life that includes pressing on—continuing to grow and struggle toward grace. He wants to be more honest about his spiritual journey. That is a longing that we would do well to share.

If we suffer from destructive spirituality and as a result are bringing fear, shame and self-reliance with us to Scripture, we need to be cautious about our abilities to "hear" what God is saying in the text. A good first step toward reclaiming Scripture is to make a careful self-examination about the ways in which Scripture has been problematic for us. What specific filters do we bring with us to the text? Can we set any of those filters aside and begin to practice expecting grace? Knowing which filters we bring with us can help us sort out the messages that come from our damaged spirituality rather than from the text.

We may find it helpful to read biblical texts in their context, reading a whole Gospel or letter or story before trying to understand what each individual verse means. It might be helpful also to read what other people have said about the text we are reading. Bible scholars have done a great deal of work over the last two millennia that can help us think about the original context and cultural nuances of the passage we are studying.

Sometimes it's easiest to begin by meditating on a phrase or short text from Scripture. Jesus' words in John 14:27, "My peace I give you," or his invitation to rest in Matthew 11:28-30 can be helpful texts to meditate on. Spending time with a phrase or a short text allows the truth to move past our fears and defenses about Scripture, so that we can hear God's voice of love speaking directly to our hearts and minds.

Most important, we would do well to practice coming to the Bible as if it actually contains good news. If we are going to see the grace that is present in Scripture, we need to set aside the filters of destructive spirituality. It is a good idea to pray before reading the Bible, asking God's Spirit to speak to our spirit and to guide us toward the grace in the text. We might say, "Help me hear the grace of your Word." Then, if something we read hurts or disturbs us, we can pray some more and trust that God will guide us in truth and grace.

Surrendering to God's love and listening to God's loving voice are practices that help us begin to live as Jesus taught us to live. These practices allow us to learn to let go of self-reliance, to let go of endless striving and to rely on God for all the help, guidance and love we need.

QUESTIONS FOR PERSONAL REFLECTION

1. What fears are you aware of that make it difficult for you to rely on God?

2. What appeals to you about self-reliance?

3. What are you anxious, angry or resentful about that you might surrender to God's care?

4. Spend some time pouring out your heart to God and then allowing yourself to be still and quiet before God, reflecting on God's love

for you. Invite God to show you God's will for you at this time. When you're ready, write about your experience in doing this.

5. As a way of practicing meditative prayer, read the words of Jesus from John 14:27: "Peace I leave with you; my peace I give you." Spend some time focusing on these words, imagining Jesus speaking them directly to you. Then reflect on this experience. What was it like for you?

9

PRACTICING HONESTY
AND HUMILITY

Surely you desire truth in the inner parts;
you teach me wisdom in the inmost place.

PSALM 51:6

Another set of tools that can help us rebuild a damaged spiritual life are those that increase our capacity for honesty and humility. These qualities are part of the soil in which we build a healthy spiritual life. Unfortunately, neither honesty nor humility seems to come instinctively to us. They are learned behaviors, and we need to practice them.

Practicing honesty and humility helps free us from fear and shame. In the chapter about spiritual abuse (chap. 1), Jeff talked about how pretense hurts us. When we are working hard to maintain an image of being superior or of being good enough, we have to keep all our struggles bottled up. This means we must struggle, by ourselves, with fear and shame—and our isolation makes things even worse. When we hide our problems, we live with the added fear that if anyone knew the truth about what goes on in our lives, they would condemn us. However, when we begin to humbly admit the truth about our struggles, we can discover that we are not alone. We can begin to experience that we are loved just as we are.

So how can we become the kind of people who have an increased capacity for honesty and humility? What disciplines will lead us in that direction? We would like to suggest several disciplines that have been helpful to us. Each of these spiritual disciplines has a long history in the Christian tradition, and we can only hint at their richness and depth. We'll explore the first three disciplines—inventory, making confession and making amends—as a set. Then we'll explore the spiritual discipline of telling our stories, sometimes called testimony. All of these practices require us to grow in our capacity to humbly recognize our defects of character and to tell the truth about them.

TAKING INVENTORY, MAKING CONFESSION AND MAKING AMENDS

The New Testament presents confession as a nonnegotiable part of the Christian life. Confession is telling the truth about ourself—about coming to the end of evasion, distraction and self-deceit. It is rarely the thing we think of first when something has gone wrong. The biblical text is clear, however, about the value of confession: "Therefore confess your sins to each other and pray for each other so that you may be healed" (James 5:16). The honest, personal confession of sins is a practice that dates back to Old Testament times and was later practiced by the early church. Confessing personal sins to and praying for each other was understood to be a vital part of experiencing grace.

Confession requires preparation, and we begin our preparations by taking an inventory. We must examine ourselves to discover the places where we are actively resisting grace. This usually involves taking a close look at our resentments, fears, selfish motives, self-reliance and the harm we have caused others. Then we need to share our findings with someone we trust. Where it is possible and appropriate, we also need to make amends for the harm we have done. This is an uncomfortable process, and it naturally brings up feelings of guilt and shame.

In the context of destructive spirituality, confession not only suffers from its natural difficulties, but it also takes place before the altar of an angry god. If we live in solidarity with gods who are harsh, impatient and shaming, then the natural discomfort of confession is exacerbated until it becomes a destructive force. Confession in such circumstances may reinforce our conviction that we are hopelessly corrupted and undeserving of God's love.

When we make our confession in the presence of the true and living God, however, we are received with open arms. Imagine that a young boy comes home from school and says to his father, "Daddy, I was mean to another kid at school today and I feel bad about it." The father doesn't scold or shame his child. Instead, he practically weeps for joy because he is so proud of his son's growing capacity for honesty and self-disclosure. He talks with his son and says, "How were you mean? What do you think you might do to make it right? It takes courage to be honest and do the right thing." If we who are damaged, struggling, missing-the-mark kinds of parents know how to respond gracefully to a child who has erred, how much more so will God respond to us in grace and love when we confess?

In a context of grace our confession can be powerful and transformative, despite its discomfort. By looking inside ourselves and making our findings known to God and to one or more trustworthy persons, we are laying a foundation of humility on which we will construct the rest of our spiritual lives. If our work here is solid, the structure will be sound.

In addition to helping us develop spiritual humility, confession takes the abstract notion that we are sinners and transforms it into a concrete reality. If we experience sin as something relatively abstract— perhaps related to misbehavior by very distant relatives (Adam and

Eve)—we probably find it difficult to connect confession with our daily lives. That is why confession must follow the process of taking a moral inventory of our lives. We need our confession to be about our lives today, not about things that happened a long time ago.

When we connect confession to our daily experiences, we grow in the knowledge that we are damaged people in need of God's grace. When we see our brokenness clearly and share it with another person, it becomes equally clear that nothing other than God's grace is sufficient to help us change; no act of self-will or strategy of self-reliance will suffice. In confession we discover brokenness, but we also discover points of contact with grace. After we make our confession, we pray that God will change us and guide us to a deeper knowledge of God's love. So we confess, we ask for help, and then it becomes possible for grace to flow into the broken places.

The spiritual discipline of confession is not a one-time experience. We need a confessional lifestyle—a way of living that is deeply open to recognizing both our shortcomings and the healing grace that is available to us as we acknowledge these shortcomings and confess them to God and to others. We can take a first step in a lifetime practice of confession by making use of a simple exercise that was first used by the nondenominational Christian movement known as the Oxford Group. This is a written exercise called the Four Absolutes.

We start by taking a piece of paper and folding it into quarters, or drawing a cross that divides the page evenly into fourths. In each section we write one of what the Oxford Group called the four absolutes: love, honesty, purity and unselfishness. These standards represent some of the qualities of Christ's life and his example to us. Then we sit quietly with these four qualities and ask God to show us where we have fallen short of them. When we get an answer, we make a note in the appropriate box.

For example, when a still, quiet voice reminds us that we shamed a friend for something we have been guilty of ourselves, we make a note of it under "honesty," since we have not been honest with our friend. Or when we are given a memory of a time when we were inconsiderate of our spouse's needs, we make a note under "love." Likewise, impurity in any relationship, including sexual and business relations or any addictive behavior would be listed under "purity," and selfish acts and motives would be listed under "unselfishness." Some items may fit into more than one category, but noting them once is enough. If we are patient and sincere in our desire for God to show us some painful truths, this exercise will unearth a good deal of material and prepare us to make confession.

Once we've made our confession, we will probably discover that we have a desire to address the harm that we have caused others. The practice of confession is intimately connected with the practice of making amends for the wrongdoing that we have confessed. Making amends for our wrongs is crucial to a healthy spiritual life and healthy relationships. The Bible puts a high value on making amends: "Therefore, if you are offering your gift at the altar and there remember that your brother has something against you, leave your gift there in front of the altar. First go and be reconciled to your brother; then come and offer your gift" (Matthew 5:23-24). Our relationship with God and with others are directly connected. We cannot be living in ways that hurt others and proceed in our relationship with God as if we have not been hurtful. How we treat others matters a great deal to God. Jesus put it simply: Loving God and loving each other are the sum total of the law. One does not exist apart from the other. Because we are human, we hurt each other. Our responsibility is to repair the hurt we have caused by addressing our error directly—and that means making amends.

At the same time it is important to be aware of ways that making amends can create harm rather than healing. It is dangerous to make amends expecting that we will get something in return. For example, if we go into this exercise asking for or demanding forgiveness, we turn our effort into something that others are supposed to do for us, rather than our confessing our wrongdoing to them. Approaching people we have hurt in the past can open their old wounds; to insist that they forgive us may exacerbate those wounds. Our job isn't to demand forgiveness from others but to acknowledge the wrong we have done and our willingness to do whatever it takes to repair the harm we have caused.

Another way we can go wrong in making amends is to not give those we've hurt the opportunity to tell us the impact that our behavior had on them. We might know what we have done to others, but it is beyond arrogant to assume that we have any idea how our behavior affected their lives. In making amends we must be ready to listen and take in whatever they want to tell us. Our goal is to approach the people we've hurt and say something like, "I know I've hurt you, and I want to make restitution. I also want to hear your experience if there is anything you need to tell me." The emphasis should not be on controlling the outcome or getting ourself off the hook, but on offering those we've hurt an opportunity to heal. They can do whatever they need to do. They might say, "You are forgiven," or they might be outraged. Their response is not our responsibility. Our job is to receive what they have to say. If we make amends with this attitude, we will learn a great deal about how our behavior affects others. We will also gain insight into what it takes for people to heal.

Alice, whose story we told in chapter four, found making amends to be an indispensable part of her rebuilding process. She had worked hard in her attempts to control her brother's and sister's spiritual lives and had completely alienated herself from them in the process. When Alice became aware of her wrongdoing and was willing to make amends, she approached her siblings and let them know not only that she knew she had been wrong and had hurt them but also that she was willing to do whatever she could to make things right. This simple confession to the people she'd harmed and the expression of willingness to make amends were the beginning of new, grace-filled relationships with her siblings. She was also building on the foundation of her new relationship with God.

A first step in making amends is to look at our previous pattern of reactions to the knowledge that we have done something wrong. Do we normally apologize and then get mad when the person we hurt doesn't immediately forgive us? Do we apologize so profusely that the other person can hardly get a word in? Do we run away? Do we deny that we've hurt anyone? Do we blame the person we have hurt or justify our behavior? Do our resentments prevent us from becoming willing to make amends? Starting to replace even a few of these unhelpful responses with the inventory-confession-amends process can make a huge difference in our capacity to experience, in practical ways, the love and grace of God.

TELLING OUR STORIES

A second major way we can practice honesty and humility is by telling our stories (sometimes called our testimony). Testimony is an honest account of our need for God's grace and of the power of God's grace to heal us. In Psalm 40:1-3, 9-10, the psalmist sings about having been in a slimy pit of mud and mire. He sings about crying out to God for help. And he sings about the gifts of grace he has received from God. He was lifted up, given a solid place to stand and a new song of gratitude and praise to sing. When the psalmist was in the slimy pit, before he called out to God, his honest testimony was that he was a mess and needed help. When he called out to God for help and was waiting for God to respond, his honest testimony was, "I am a mess, I have called out for God's help, and I am waiting." And when the psalmist experienced God's help, his honest testimony was an expression of gratitude and praise. Testimony is the truthful sharing of our experiences as they unfold—including our struggles, doubts, pain and gratitude for grace and healing when they come.

Testimony becomes distorted when we think that it is always supposed to make us—or God—look good. In some parts of the Christian community, a good testimony is understood to sound like this: "I was bad and sad. Then I found Jesus, and now I am good and glad." Often we craft "good" testimonies of this kind because we think that people will be attracted to this idealized image. We are tempted to give a good testimony because we believe we are supposed to project an image of purity and perfection that shows other people just how great our God is. So "good" testimonies tend to leave out certain key elements of our story. We tend not to mention all the dead ends in our lives, all the two-steps-forward-and-one-step-back events, all the wandering-in-the-wilderness parts. And leaving out those key elements, frankly, tends to make good testimony boring, one-dimensional and, in the end, unbelievable. Even worse, such a testimony can become a source of spiritual shame and discouragement for people who know that their lives are not nearly as good or ideal as we are making ours sound.

What is necessary in the spiritual rebuilding process is not a "good" but an honest testimony. We need to learn to tell the truth. If our testimony is not the truth, it has no spiritual benefit for us or for anyone else. Testimony must include the messy, untidy, confusing and emotionally painful parts. We are not perfect. Our lives are not squeaky clean. We get depressed. We struggle with shame. When we give honest testimony, we state our brokenness clearly and explain exactly what we are struggling with today.

Those of us who have spent many years giving good testimony are probably feeling uneasy about all this truth telling. "The truth is good," we will admit, "but how can airing our dirty laundry in public attract people to Jesus or to the church?" In response to this reaction, Juanita has a story to tell about a Christian friend who hadn't attended church in many years.

> I invited my friend to come with me to church one Sunday. At that time we were attending a church that was quite perfor-mance-oriented. It was a church where only "good" testimonies were given. These were testimonies that glossed over pain and struggle, and sounded too easy to be true. My friend's response after the service was to say, "What a wonderful church! But I could never be like these people. Their spiritual lives sound easy and they all look so good." Our church had been putting on a show, pretending to be good Christians without problems. In the process, we were actually alienating people, because what we were doing was not honest or humble.

What we tend to call good testimony is denial, plain and sim-ple. Any spirituality that is based on denial is a spirituality that is based on lies, and it quickly becomes a destructive force. As bro-ken people, we doubt. We have trouble trusting. We don't have all the answers. We hurt, and we hurt others. We harbor resent-ments and pride and greed. But as soon as we are honest about the brokenness of our spiritual lives, we will have people on the edge of their seats, saying, "These people are like me! Maybe I can get help here."

Being honest about our lives involves more than just telling the truth about the difficult parts of our lives. We also need to tell the truth about our growing capacity to experience the love and grace of God. Testimony is especially effective and useful when it is deeply grounded in our experience of grace. We need to tell the truth about whatever grace we have actually experienced. When we can talk about a personal crisis and how God is helping us through it, we offer hope to others in the midst of similar crises. When we are in the middle of struggling with temptation or destructive impulses and are drawing strength from God, we can tell the truth about that; we can testify to the power of God's grace in the midst of the struggle. If we've been given a daily reprieve from addictive obsession, we can testify about that. If we are struggling to find a grace-filled pathway through a divorce, we can testify with gratitude that we still have hope that grace will guide us. Even if we are feeling lost and don't know what to do except wait for God to guide us, we can testify to the hope that empowers us to tolerate the waiting. No matter what we are going through, the grace of God is there. And we can testify to the ways we are experiencing that grace.

Honest testimony, then, is about our human struggle and about God's grace. It is an expression of our pain and of our genuine gratitude. When we share our pain and then encounter God's help, we feel deep gratitude. When, like the psalmist, we have acknowledged our experiences in the "mud and mire" and then later find our feet on "solid rock," the spontaneous gratitude we feel is a direct experience of grace, which can become a true gift to others.

Bethany, whose story we told in chapter one, continued in her support group long after her daughter had stopped using drugs. In the group, Bethany found not only support for her own struggles but a place where she could serve others by sharing her own story honestly. She spoke of her hardships as a parent of a drug addict. She spoke of the tools she had learned for rebuilding her spiritual life even while her daughter was still using drugs. And she shared her deep gratitude for the grace she was experiencing for the first time in her life. Because this kind of testimony was so nourishing to her, Bethany also started another support group, one for people who had experienced spiritual abuse. By giving honest testimony about her own experience as a spiritual abuser and her ongoing struggles to stay free of abusive spirituality, Bethany was able to bring hope and strength to many who had suffered from spiritual abuse or who, like herself, were spiritual abusers working to rebuild their spiritual lives.

As a first step toward practicing testimony, it is probably not a good idea to tell our story in front of a large group. We can choose one person or a small group of people with whom we feel comfortable enough to be honest. Without preparing what we are going to say, or withholding anything to make ourselves look less broken than we are, we can talk about our current experience of life and of God as honestly as possible. Give it a try. See how it goes. Create an environment of honest testimony and let the circle expand to include others. Welcome anyone who wants to hear and speak some truth, and see what the Holy Spirit will do.

QUESTIONS FOR PERSONAL REFLECTION

1. What experiences have you had with inventory, confession and making amends?

2. Try the exercise of folding a blank piece of paper into fourths and writing one of the four absolutes—love, purity, unselfishness and honesty—in each square. Ask God to lovingly show you where you

are missing the mark in any or all of these areas. Write down whatever comes to your attention.

3. Write a brief, honest testimony of your current spiritual situation and experience.

4. Share this testimony with at least one person you trust.

10

LIVING IN COMMUNITY

Two are better than one,

> *because they have a good return for their work:*

If one falls down,

> *his friend can help him up.*
> *But pity the man who falls*
> *and has no one to help him up!*

ECCLESIASTES 4:9-10

Participating in community allows us to discover that we are not alone in our struggle with fear, shame and spiritual brokenness. Community gives us a place to hear other people's stories of struggle and grace, and to share our own unfolding stories. Community is a place where we can practice honesty and humility, and where we can give and receive gifts of strength and hope. For all these reasons, we need community as we rebuild our damaged spiritual lives.

We may often be tempted to choose isolation over community, and isolation is the soil in which many kinds of spiritual dysfunction take root. Our isolation can be driven by fears, as we discussed in chapter seven, or by a kind of toxic self-reliance that is out of touch with our need for community. Whatever the reason, isolation is not in our best interests. It is not good for us to be alone. All our self-destructive actions and self-defeating ideas are things we learned in dysfunctional relationships, and we will not become healthier people until we build healthier, more grace-filled relationships in which we practice new ways of relating.

RECOGNIZING TRUE FELLOWSHIP

Not all social experiences provide the kind of fellowship we need. Most of us know what it is like to be surrounded by people but to feel profoundly alone. Regardless of the specifics of our spiritual struggles, we know that superficial social niceties or interactions that don't go past "How are you?" and "Fine, thanks" will not help us. When we try to replace true fellowship with mere socializing, we may end up feeling emotionally drained and discouraged. Each of us longs for a community where we can be honest about the spiritual struggles we experience. If our faith community gives us the message that it is not okay to be struggling, each of us will think we are the only one in the community who struggles. We will feel isolated. There is an appropriate place for coffee and doughnuts, and there is an appropriate time for saying hello and chatting about the weather and sports and whatever. We do not need all our relationships to have honesty, vulnerability and transparency as the highest priority. But we do need a safe place, perhaps several places, where we can be our authentic selves. Recognizing these places and growing in our ability to create such places are some of the most important things we need in the process of rebuilding our spiritual lives.

The first and perhaps most important question to ask about any community when we are in the rebuilding process is whether this is a safe and supportive place to do what we need to do in rebuilding our spiritual lives. In order to answer this question, there are a few characteristics that are almost always useful to check for.

Confidentiality versus gossip. Communities that understand the importance of confidentiality are almost certainly more helpful than those that do not. We cannot say what we need to say unless we know that the people who hear us have a capacity for confidentiality. If gossip is a common practice in a community—in spite of how sharply it's condemned in the Bible—there is no way for that community to be safe for us. A safe community, of any size, is one that can maintain condidentiality. A small support group works best when things that are said in the group are not repeated elsewhere.

Identification versus advice. Unless we ask for advice, we probably don't want it—and won't benefit from it. What is much more helpful is to interact with people who can identify with our struggle sufficiently to offer hope. It is always appropriate for people to present their own stories about difficult experiences and how they overcame them with God's help. But this does not mean they should preach or grandstand or deliver long lectures. We need people who can identify ways in which they have experienced what we are experiencing and who can humbly share their experience when it might be helpful.

The importance of identification is illustrated by a story Dale tells about a woman—we'll call her Mary—who was in a twelve-step group he once visited. When it was Mary's turn to share, she started to cry. And she kept on crying for the full amount of time allotted for each person to share. Here's how Dale describes the experience:

> It was moving. It was clear that she was doing the work she had come to do that night. It was painful work. And it took courage to do it. I was sitting there remembering the times in my own life when I had no words, when the pain was just too overwhelming for words. I identified. It brought a tear to my eye as well, as I remembered those times and the intimations of grace that

I could now see were lurking about even in the darkest hours. But I was also aware that Mary's tears were creating anxiety for some people in the group. I was a guest in the group that night and, probably because I was there, the pastor decided to come as well. I could feel his anxiety increase as Mary continued to weep. Eventually he couldn't take it any more and said, "We should pray for Mary."

You might be able to guess what happened immediately. First, Mary stopped crying. Instead of being in a room of people whose job was to identify with her in her suffering, she was in a room of people who were anxiously focused on her. It no longer felt safe to share, so she stopped. The other thing I noticed was that I immediately stopped doing the work that I needed to do that night. Instead of working on my own painful memories and reflecting on the intimations of God's grace that I was now beginning to see, I was focused elsewhere. Of course, in any other kind of group—a Bible study, a Sunday school class and so on—the pastor's suggestion would have been understood to be a caring and helpful suggestion. But in the social context of this group, it was a significant violation of the group norms, because it got in the way of our ability to identify with another person's story and to allow that person to share.

Identification is given a very high priority in the dynamics of twelve-step groups. People in recovery from addiction or codependency have learned from difficult experiences the importance of having robust boundaries about not giving advice, not asking questions and not making comments about other people's stories during the group time. It is all too easy to focus on other people rather than on the work we ourselves need to do. Jesus' teaching about the speck of sawdust and the plank seem relevant to us in this context (Matthew 7:3-5). Imagine what a group would look like if every group member took Jesus' teaching seriously and showed up ready to work on their own planks rather than on other people's specks of sawdust!

Responsibility versus blame. Communities that focus on other people's sins rather than on their own sins are not likely to be very helpful to us. We need places where each group member takes responsibility for his or her own behavior and feelings. A healthy group is not a place to blame other people for our actions or emotions. Each of us must take responsibility for ourselves if we want to grow in our capacity to receive grace.

Shared leadership versus authoritarian leadership. Most safe groups operate on level ground. No one gets to pass laws or create rules of conduct for others. Decisions are made as a group, and members encourage each other to adhere to mutual commitments. By merit of their experience of personal change, some group members will have wisdom to offer. And because they are relatively new, other members will have a greater need. It is natural for need to look to experience for guidance. But it is abusive if experienced members insist that new members follow their demands. We are all God's children, each as broken and as loved as the next. Group dynamics should reflect this reality.

Grace versus judgment. Being in relationship with others offers us a continuous opportunity either to pass judgment or to receive and extend grace. We each have our own wounds, our own perspectives, our own thoughts and feelings. These differences can lead to misunderstandings, and they can seduce us into being critical and judgmental of each other. Or they can be opportunities to love and be loved, to accept our differences, to value each other and to listen to each other with respect.

To foster grace-filled communication we need to practice grace toward each other. The apostle Paul described some of the specifics of what it means to practice grace: "Be completely humble and gentle; be patient, bearing with one another in love. Make every effort to keep the unity of the Spirit through the bond of peace" (Ephesians 4:2-3). When a group practices these guidelines over a considerable period of time, its participants become increasingly interested in working for change. They are able to open up and share their struggles, and grow in their desire to receive grace. It is important to remember that just as we do not need a perfect therapist, a perfect sponsor or a perfect pastor, we do not need a perfect community—just one that is a reasonably safe place for us to do what we need to do to take the next steps in the rebuilding process.

In chapter two we told the story of Ted, who was resistant to receiving God's love and grace. Ted couldn't bring himself to trust that such love was really available, and even hearing a sermon about receiving from God was too much for him. However, Ted was persuaded to join a small group for people like him, people who struggled to receive spiritual food. Ted's group was a safe place: what was said in that group stayed in that group; its members were loving and patient; they could express their feelings and also gain insight into their resistance to God's love and grace; and they did not demand anything of Ted, but offered him a space to have his own experience and to share only if he felt the desire. Because of the severity of his spiritual anorexia, Ted was unable to gain the full benefit of this spiritual community. The grace in the group was more than he could handle at that point in his rebuilding process. Even so, when Ted left the group (and his church), he left with a seed planted in his spirit. His spiritual anorexia had been confronted in a direct and loving manner, and he had renounced his attachment to a false, distant god. The seed planted by the loving grace of this small group eventually flowered into a more complete recovery for Ted. It took time, but he did eventually learn to receive from God, in small doses, the grace he had refused for so long.

A first step toward fellowship is to ask for God's guidance as we either join a group or—if no appropriate group is available—start a new one. It is important for us to realize that we are not the only struggling people in our faith communities. Even if all the other members of our church appear to be happy all the time, the truth is that most people have the same struggles and need for honest fellowship that we have. So if we sense that God is leading us to start a new group, we might begin by getting together with a few interested, trustworthy people and practicing some of the tools described in this book. You might find it helpful to create a list based on the guidelines we have just discussed and read them aloud at the beginning of each meeting. At a minimum, such a list might include the following:

1. Anything said in the group is considered confidential and will not be discussed outside the group unless specific permission is given to do so.

2. We will provide time for each person present to talk if he or she feels comfortable doing so.

3. We will talk about ourselves and our own situations, avoiding conversation about other people.

4. We will listen attentively to each other.

5. We will refrain from giving advice.

6. We will ask God to give us the courage we need to be honest and humble in doing the work we need to do as we listen and as we share.

7. We will ask for God's help in being open to receive and to extend grace as we listen and as we share.

Before long, we will want to make our group available to others who want to give it a try. People will come and go, and in time a core group will develop and grow. Then we will have formed a place where people can come and be honest about their lives. We will be part of a group where everyone present can experience grace.

PRACTICING SPIRITUAL PARTNERSHIP

Fellowship is important because it is not good for us to be alone. But we need more than fellowship. We also need counsel. The biblical text is clear about this:

> Plans fail for lack of counsel,
> but with many advisers they succeed. (Proverbs 15:22)

We need the wisdom of others who have gone ahead of us in life's journey. We do not have to learn everything by trial and error. In the spiritual life it is appropriate for those of us with less experience to turn to those with more experience and ask for guidance.

Sometimes our needs for spiritual partnership are met naturally as part of the life of a community. It is much more common, however, for us to need a one-to-one relationship of some kind, at least for a while, for a spiritual partnership to work well. There are many names for the kind of person we need in a spiritual partnership: spiritual director, counselor, pastor, spiritual friend, mentor, sponsor and so on. We will use the term *partner* to designate the person we choose to help us learn how to apply the core tools of the Christian faith to our spiritual lives. We have selected this term because it emphasizes that both parties are in the process of rebuilding their spiritual lives. Spiritual partners understand that they also are broken and in need of help. Partnership ought to provide a safe environment for self-examination, honesty and change. We need someone who can hear our deepest confession without judgment, someone who won't minimize our struggle. We need a partner who can help us remember to rely on God rather than on our own efforts, and who can mirror back to us our mistakes in a supportive way.

The practice of spiritual partnership can become distorted by destructive spirituality in many ways. Partners who take a position of superiority rather than of support cause harm. The result is that we no longer feel safe enough to be honest. Rather than reminding us to rely on God's grace and guidance, abusive partners communicate that we should rely on them and their advice. This dynamic is as lethal for partners as it is for us, because in placing themselves in a superior position their own self-reliance is reinforced, deepening their resistance to grace.

Another common distortion of spiritual partnership is one that focuses solely on behavior. If we have a partner who focuses strictly on accountability for our behavior and offers nothing more than encouragement to try harder to control our actions, the relationship will not likely help us much. Trying harder might actually work for minor behavioral adjustments, but for the problems we're talking about in this book, extra effort only makes things worse. The problem is that the self-reliance embedded in the imperative to try harder keeps us divorced from the experience of relying on God and on God's grace. And without practical access to grace, we end up with a heap of shame on top of our existing problems. Focusing on our own efforts to change our behavior expresses a lack of openness to what God wants to do in our lives.

You might remember Eric, whose story we told in chapter three. When Eric attended his first Alcoholics Anonymous meeting, he met Bob, who impressed Eric as someone whose relationship with God was full of compassion and grace. On a daily basis God was doing things for Bob that Bob couldn't do for himself. When Eric first met with Bob, Eric found him to be kind and humble, never giving orders or making demands. Bob simply offered Eric his personal experiences that related to Eric's struggles. Bob showed Eric what he had done to rebuild his own relationship with God and made himself available to help Eric through the process if he wanted to give it a try. So Eric asked Bob to be his spiritual partner. During the course of their relationship Eric was able to take suggestions from Bob, and those suggestions led Eric through most of the tools we describe in this book. As a result, Eric's spirituality was rebuilt on solid ground.

The role of our spiritual partner is to meet with us on a regular basis, to listen to the honest confession of our inventory, help us reflect on our struggles with understanding and respect, and listen to and celebrate our experiences of grace and growth. Spiritual partners might also share from their own experiences, offering points of identification and wisdom. They speak the truth in love to us about areas where we are still blind to what we are doing. Most important, our spiritual partners remind us that the work we need to do can be done only as we learn to surrender our lives to God's loving care. Again and again, our spiritual partners call us back from the exhausting path of self-reliant striving to the light burdens that Jesus promised his followers (Matthew 11:30). In all these ways the relationship with our spiritual partners can offer us both a safe place to practice honesty and spiritual humility, and a regular source of spiritual nurture, encouragement, wisdom and grace.

When spiritual partnership is based on helping a person find grace, and when it is supportive rather than abusive, it can help our growth immensely. It reminds us that we are not alone. It provides us with the hard-earned wisdom of someone who has suffered from similar destructive dynamics and who is further along in the process of reconstruction than we are. If we start construction without an experienced guide, we run the risk of constructing yet another building on the same faulty foundation.

A first step toward finding a spiritual partner is to pray for guidance. We can start by asking God to bring someone into our lives—or to give us the eyes to see someone who is already present and available. It can also be helpful to ask others for recommendations. We might want to interview potential spiritual partners, asking how they see such a relationship, if they have done this before. Such conversations can give us a sense of whether this person might be a good fit for our needs. We need someone who already has practiced these tools for spiritual reconstruction with a spiritual partner, and we need someone who feels safe and with whom we can be fully honest, so that God's grace can touch us and bring healing in our lives.

The rebuilding of our spiritual lives on God's grace needs to take place in the context of relationship with others who have been rebuilding or are seeking to rebuild their lives on grace. Being part of a group or a partnership offers us opportunities to take in from others and to share with others the wisdom and hope we need for the rebuilding process. We can find courage and offer hope as we listen to and share the struggles of life and the surprising encounters with grace that come along the way.

QUESTIONS FOR PERSONAL REFLECTION

1. What experiences have you had with faith communities and spiritual partnerships that were not safe? What made the experience less than safe?

2. What experiences have you had with faith communities and spiritual partnerships that were safe and nurturing? What made them safe and nurturing?

3. What do you need in terms of community at this time in your life?

4. What could be done to create a safe group in your faith community?

5. What could be done to provide safe spiritual mentors or partners in your faith community?

11

GIVING BACK

*Be imitators of God, therefore, as dearly loved children and live a life
of love, just as Christ loved us.*

EPHESIANS 5:1-2

The central dynamic of the spiritual rebuilding process is growth in
our capacity to receive God's love and grace. While these gifts of love
and grace are for us, they are not for us only. They are given to us so
that we can pass them on. If we have received love, passing it on does
not diminish what we have left. The love and grace of God are not in
short supply; there is plenty to go around. We will still have all the love
and grace we can hold, no matter how much we give away. And we do
not need to wait before we pass on what we are receiving. As soon as
there is growth in our capacity to receive the love and grace of God,
we can begin looking for practical ways to share these gifts with others.
So passing on to others the gifts we are receiving from God is one final
tool set that is essential to rebuilding a damaged spiritual life.

There are lots of ways to pass on what we have been given. The
spiritual discipline of testimony, which we talked about in chapter
nine, is one way to share with others the experience we are having
with God and the strength and hope that is growing within us as a
result. Making amends and being a safe person in our faith community

are also ways that God's grace flows into us and through us. In this chapter we focus on two additional spiritual disciplines: forgiveness and service. Both are ways that we can share with others the love and grace of God we are experiencing.

FORGIVENESS

The Gospels are full of Jesus' teachings on the power and importance of forgiveness. "If someone strikes you on the right cheek, turn . . . the other also" (Matthew 5:39). Rather than retaliate or become resentful, we are to forgive. It is important to notice that Jesus did not make this statement to an audience full of victims of domestic violence. He was speaking to the Pharisees. The Greek word for *strike* used in this passage means an insulting slap, a light and disgracing blow to the cheek. To get at the heart of Jesus' statement, we have to ask ourselves what it would take for a Pharisee to respond to that kind of slap in the manner Jesus suggests. The Pharisees are presented in Matthew's Gospel as people who falsely boosted their egos by presenting themselves as pure and perfect followers of God's law. They were religious leaders, people with power, who saw themselves as spiritually superior to others. Rather than living lives of honesty and humility, they were living lives of pretense and pride, and in doing so they were spiritually abusing others. Jesus' criticism of these people is clear; he calls them whitewashed tombs—clean on the outside but rotting within. For such a person to forgive someone who publicly insults him by slapping his face, the Pharisee would have to let go of all his religious pretense, all his ego-boosting lies and self-reliance, all his attachment to false spiritual superiority. He would have to learn to love his assailant as someone who is a broken and beloved child of God—and therefore his equal.

It is easy to confuse forgiveness with other things, and sometimes the confusion can make us more fearful of forgiving someone. So it's worth clarifying what forgiveness does not mean.

Forgiveness has nothing to do with approving of the harmful actions of others. Forgiving others does not mean that what they did was okay. It does mean that we are asking God to free us from our resentments. Stewing on the things that have happened to us, torturing ourselves by replaying events over and over again in our minds brings neither justice nor retribution. Doing this only leaves us exhausted, depressed and irritable. Forgiveness is a pathway, a process, that leads us to freedom from resentments.

Forgiveness has nothing to do with pretending. We don't have to pretend that past wrongs don't hurt and that we are all better now. Forgiveness is not saying, "Everything is okay now." Forgiveness is just the opposite of pretending; it is about telling the truth. The truth is that if I try to carry these resentments by myself, the load will kill me. So I need to give these resentments to someone who is able to do the heavy lifting—someone with a lot of real-life experience with forgiveness— which brings us back to Jesus. Jesus made forgiveness a priority, and it is not a priority that he arrived at by some sort of theoretical reflection. His life was full of opportunities for resentment and bitterness, yet he practiced forgiveness. And if we take the biblical text seriously, Jesus is available to do the heavy lifting for us, the lifting we cannot do for ourselves.

Forgiveness is not the same as reconciliation. Forgiveness does not mean that our relationship is restored to the condition it was in before an offense occurred. We don't have to stay in relationship with people who have hurt us unless they are committed to change and are making real, observable progress in becoming less abusive.

Forgiveness has nothing to do with forgetting. Trying hard to forget is almost never a successful way to gain freedom from resentment. The reason is simple: forgetting is not based on honesty. Forgetting asks us to deny the truth of our experience and to do so by virtue of great personal effort. Trying hard to forget is a strategy not only of denial but of self-will and self-reliance. In Matthew 18:22 Jesus responds to a question about forgiveness by saying we should forgive "seventy times seven" (RSV). Read through the lens of distorted spirituality, Jesus seems to be proposing that we run a forgiveness supermarathon, making 70 x 7 (490) laps around the same issue before we finally let go of our resentments. We would propose, instead, that in this text, Jesus is encouraging us to come to a place inside ourselves that feels like lap 490—a place where we are so exhausted by our attempts to forgive and forget on our own power that there isn't anything left for us to do but turn our resentments over to God. Forgetting is not the key to freedom from resentment. The key is to come to the end of our efforts to forget and to surrender our resentments to a God who we know values both justice and compassion.

When the wounds we have experienced run deep and we have been investing all our energy in forgiveness strategies that are not helpful, it's easy for us to become stuck in the role of victim. Over the years the defensiveness and anger we feel can come to define our personalities. Rather than an event that we experienced, the hurtful act and its effects become who we are. This makes it difficult to let go of resentment. Because we cannot imagine life without resentment, we come to believe that the effects of the wrongs done to us are permanent, that healing grace is impossible in this area of our lives. When we become a "victim," we also cast those who hurt us in the role of offender. Just as we are hopelessly locked into a single role, they also become one-dimensional people, so that we can think of them only in terms of how they have hurt us. Unable to allow for the possibility of their humanity, we convince ourselves that they are completely unlike us, and we tell ourselves that they deserve pain and suffering. We cannot believe that a just God would allow such people any taste of grace.

By casting ourselves and the people who hurt us in these polarized roles, we create a lie that effectively blocks us from experiencing God's healing love for us. The truth is that all of us are broken people who act poorly and have a deep need of grace. In order to forgive, we need to ask God to help us get in touch with our own brokenness and with God's love for us. If we can stay in touch with God's compassion for us, God's tenderness for the broken places in us and God's forgiveness for the ways we have gotten in the way of our own healing, then forgiving others may flow out of that received grace. When we see the truth of our condition, we see that what we believed to be permanent damage is not permanent at all. No one can hurt us so deeply as to separate us from grace. Although sin is hurtful, it is ultimately powerless because God's love is stronger than all the sin and pain in this world. As we grow in our ability to receive the grace and love of God, we may also find that we are growing in our ability to see those who hurt us as our damaged, broken, missing-the-mark brother or sister—loved dearly by the same God who loves us.

Juanita's experience of healing from childhood abuse helps to illustrate this process. Here's how she talks about it:

> I remember clearly the day I experienced God speaking to me about this. "I want to heal you," I sensed God saying. "I want to take away all the shame and despair and fear that you carry. It is because I can heal your shame and fear that you can forgive the wrongs that were done to you."
>
> For an instant I thought: *What an amazing offer! What an incredible gift!* I fully expected to hear myself responding with a clear, grateful yes. But instead, I hesitated. I fought with myself, say-

ing, *Wait a minute. Wait! Who will I be without this shame, this rage, this despair, this fear?*

I could not hear any answer to this question at the time. The question hung in the air. *Who will I be if I am not consumed with shame? Who will I be if fear does not rule my life? Who will remember the wrong done to me if my rage subsides? How will life make sense without my despair?* I had no answers to these questions.

Fortunately, over time, answers have come. Who will I be if I live in the freedom of healing and forgiveness? I will be myself, my true self, the person I have always really been—God's own deeply loved child. What we are saying about ourselves when we consider stepping into the fullness of healing and forgiveness is that no matter what has been done to us, even though people have treated us as if we were not lovable or valuable, the truth is that we are loved and valued. We are saying that even though we have been victimized, these events do not tell us who we are. We are acknowledging that no matter how badly we were treated, we are—and always have been—beloved children of God.

When I experienced release from the shame I carried, I was able to release those who had harmed me. The harm was real, but it was not permanent. It could be undone. I could be healed. Forgiveness was a kind of byproduct of this release from shame, rather than something I had to generate within myself by self-will or determination.

A good first step toward forgiveness is to honestly acknowledge our hurt and resentment and then to ask for grace to pray for the people we resent. As God gives us the grace to pray, we begin to see, in the light of God's love, those who have hurt us being released from the things that imprison them. We might also pray for ourselves and see ourselves released from the harm their actions caused us.

When we remember Christ's death and resurrection, we remember Jesus, who prayed for those who were hurting him, "Father, forgive them, for they do not know what they are doing" (Luke 23:34). The attempts to demean and destroy Jesus were ultimately futile. The abuse he suffered did not change who Jesus was or Jesus' love for those who hurt him.

You might recall that Ted, who struggled with spiritual anorexia, left his support group and his church in a fit of resentments. He had deep, lifelong resentments against his parents and saw no reason to forgive them. Although the resentments caused him great suffering and turmoil, and caused him to leave the support of his group and his church, Ted held on to those resentments with all his might. It wasn't until some time later, in another church, that Ted was able to hear the words of the gospel that he needed to hear. Christ's words from the cross penetrated the fog of Ted's resentments and gave him an entirely new perspective on his situation with his parents. Set free from his resentments, Ted was free to continue rebuilding his spiritual life on the solid foundation of grace.

SERVICE

One of the dangers of a spiritual reconstruction project is that we can get so focused on the project that we neglect those around us. For that reason it is important to remember that the purpose of this whole adventure is not just private and personal. While we hope to experience deep, fundamental personal change, we are not in this only for ourselves.

One important way that we can pass on some of the grace we are experiencing as we rebuild our spiritual lives is through acts of service. As with all the other tools we have talked about, service can be distorted by dysfunctional spirituality. For example, it can become self-serving. We can engage in service as a way to distract ourselves from the problems in our family or in our own spiritual lives. Service also has a way of allowing us to feel superior to those we serve. Because we are the ones giving, we can use service to put ourselves in a position of power and control. Any time we place ourselves over the people we serve, we do harm both to them and to ourselves. Even as we give of our time and energy, the message we communicate is that the people we serve are less important or more broken than we are. This feeling of superiority is deadly to us spiritually, because it feeds our denial about our own needs, separates us from our own brokenness, and leaves us less able to receive the grace we need.

The goal of service is not to communicate superiority to those we serve, but to come from underneath, to support them and lift them up. Compassion means that we feel with others and care about them in their situations. To do this we must acknowledge the full humanity of others. We need to learn to see them as God's beloved children. When we can extend this kind of love and respect to others, we act as mirrors of God's grace to them.

Our first step toward service is determined by whether we are doing any service now. If we are already spending a lot of time and energy helping others, we might want our first step to be fasting from service for a while, so that we can make an accurate assessment of the role that service plays in our lives. Here are some questions we can ask ourselves:

- Are we hurting anyone (including ourselves) by not setting limits on how much we do?

- Is our service hurting us spiritually?

- Are we doing our service to make ourselves feel important?

- Are we doing our service to try to earn value in the eyes of God?
- Do we see a need to control others being exhibited in any of our efforts to be helpful?

We need to get clear answers to these questions before we try to engage in service. If our efforts to be of service lead us to exhaustion or resentments, we are likely having trouble receiving grace in the context of service. If this is our situation, we may need to extend our abstinence—take a leave of absence—from service for a period of time. This can feel like disobedience or spiritual failure, but we need to do whatever is necessary to ensure that service results in a grace-filled, lightly burdened life.

If we are not engaged in any service, our first step might be to ask God for guidance. Some of us dread service because we think it means doing something that makes us feel awkward and uncomfortable. Jeff tells a story about a member of his congregation who was initially resistant to the idea of service as part of his spiritual rebuilding project.

A man came to me for counsel—I'll call him Joe—and as we spoke, Joe said he didn't want to do any kind of service for others in the congregation or the community. I said, "I think you do, Joe. Why else would you come in here and tell me about it?" He said that even though some part of him might be willing to help out, a larger part of him thought that service was going to make him uncomfortable. He didn't want to do evangelism or visit people in the hospital or anything of the kind. So I asked him what he liked to do in his spare time, and he said he liked to go fishing.

"Well, Joe," I said, "There are a number of kids in our congregation who have no one to take them fishing on weekends. How would you feel about organizing a small team of people to take these kids fishing?"

Joe was startled. "Would that count?" he asked. The next week, he began a fishing club. That was many years ago, and Joe is still running his fishing club today.

Joe's love of fishing and his service to those kids were a perfect match. We probably cannot expect that all service will be this kind of perfect fit. But we can see a general truth here. The person doing the serving receives grace, just as the person being helped receives grace, and so the person doing the serving is just as empowered as the person being served. Grace is the key to the whole matter. When we give back we experience God's grace flowing into us and then, through us, to others. The practices of forgiveness and service are two key ways that we can open ourselves to this flow of grace.

QUESTIONS FOR PERSONAL REFLECTION

1. What difficulties have you had with forgiving someone who hurt you?

2. What grace have you experienced in forgiving or in being forgiven?

3. Reread the personal assessment questions about the place of service in your life (pp. 181-82). What dynamics are you aware of that might be problematic for you and for those you serve?

4. What acts of service that you have done, or that you have received, have been especially meaningful to you?

5. Ask God to give you the wisdom, guidance and humility to be of service to others at this time in your life.

12

NEXT STEPS

Ultimately, we don't heal, transform, or create ourselves. We posture ourselves in ways that allow God to heal, transform, and create us.

SUE MONK KIDD

Our search for more grace-filled ways to relate to God may mean a lot of change, and even good change is often difficult. Any spiritual rebuilding project is difficult, complex and time-consuming. The process of demolishing our unstable spiritual foundations can leave us feeling exposed and vulnerable, and we may at times experience fear and shame, which can be deeply painful.

We wish we could offer you a pathway to a stable, healthy spiritual life that is less painful, less complex, less demanding and less time-consuming. But we hope it is clear by now that the process described in this book is radically preferable to putting another coat of fresh paint on a building that is ready to collapse. No matter how difficult the rebuilding process may be, it is far easier than continuing on with pretense, denial, self-reliance and religious striving. Those things lead to exhaustion, resentments, discouragement and a sense of alienation from God. The difficult process of rebuilding a damaged spiritual life is like rest for our souls compared to the impossible demands that come from shame-based spirituality.

We also hope it is clear that rebuilding a damaged spiritual life is possible. It can be done. Our hopeful assessment of what is possible does not come from any optimism about our abilities to be good enough, smart enough, dedicated enough, committed enough, spiritual enough or anything enough to get the job done. It comes instead from a conviction about God. There is hope for rebuilding our damaged spiritual lives because the living and true God is actively engaged with us in the rebuilding process. The whole process hinges on God doing the things that only God can do.

This is really good news. There are lots of places in the process where we might be tempted to give up. But God is relentless in pursuing us with love; God does not give up. There are times when we might be overcome with shame. But God does not add to our shame; instead, God seeks to comfort us and help us see ways that our brokenness might become an occasion for blessing. There are times when we might feel that we are just too damaged and that the process might be a waste of time. But God does not forget how precious we are; God is patient, kind and compassionate. In all these ways, and many others, God not only sees the rebuilding process more clearly than we do but is more committed to the process than we are. And that is really good news.

It takes a great deal of courage to rest in the grace of God. Letting go of our efforts to control life and easing into the idea that God is a good, faithful and loving God is uncomfortable for most of us. We become anxious and we obsess about all the things that might go wrong if we don't do something about them. We may find ourselves thinking, *If God doesn't come through, the results will be disastrous, and it will be all my fault for letting go.* However, we know from experience that when we entrust ourselves and others into the loving hands of God, our fear is diminished and grace comes through. We hope that this book has given you some useful suggestions about how to test the reality of God's grace as a foundation for your spiritual life.

CHOOSING THE NEXT STEP

You might experience our encouragement to entrust your life to God's loving care as a call to passivity. But it is actually a call to action. It is not, however, a call to action based on self-reliance. The kind of action we have been describing as important to spiritual reconstruction is grounded in reliance on God. We ask for guidance, we listen to God's voice and to the voice of wise counsel, and then, with God's light showing us the next step and God's Spirit giving us the grace and help we need, we take that next step. We are no longer striving to get things right—trying hard, trying harder or trying our hardest. Rather, in the words of the prophet Micah, we "walk humbly" with our God (Micah 6:8), one step at a time, step after step.

The question, then, is what would be a good next step for you?

It is difficult to generalize about this topic, because each person's spiritual journey is unique. The next action step for you to take might be to become more educated about one of the spiritual disciplines we have talked about in this book. Many books about spiritual disciplines have been published, and we have included a short bibliography that might be a useful starting point for you if you think this is the next action step to take.

We encourage you, however, not to just read another book. If becoming really educated about the rebuilding process were the key to a successful outcome, the whole process would be much easier. But it takes more than book learning to build a house. For that reason we want to emphasize the importance of taking action. Some aspects of the spiritual rebuilding process can be learned only by putting ideas into practice. We can learn about prayer by reading about prayer, but we can't be changed by it until we do it. We can learn about making amends by reading about it, but we can't experience the terrifying goodness of making amends until we take concrete, real-world steps to do it.

Jesus told a story about the importance of taking action (Matthew 21:28-32). A farmer had two sons, and one day he asked both sons to help him out by working in the fields. One son said he would help, but he never showed up. The other son said he would not help, but he showed up to do the work. Which son, asked Jesus, did what his father wanted? It's a good question. Clearly, talking the talk was not what Jesus was trying to encourage. The importance of action—doing something, no matter how small, no matter how imperfect—is one of the main lessons we've learned from our own spiritual rebuilding projects.

We realize we've covered a lot of ground in this book. It would certainly not be helpful to try to put all the ideas in this book into action at once. Healing takes time, and so our work toward healing should be gradual. We suggest that you choose one thing you felt strongly about while reading this book, and try to find a way to put it into action. Perhaps you felt a strong call to make amends when we discussed that practice, or perhaps you felt a need to practice surrendering to God. Reread that part of the book, and then do whatever you need to do to begin putting it into practice.

You might be terrified by the prospect of making substantive changes in your spiritual life. While we may admit that there are problems in our relationship with God, the idea of making major changes in the nature of that relationship can feel daunting; we may not know if we have the strength to begin. If you identify with these fears, we suggest moving slowly and not expecting yourself to do more than you are able. But move. Slow is fine, but do something. We recommend that you change one thing, no matter how small, and let that change stay with you for a while before you try anything else. We believe you will notice that even very small changes can have a systemic effect in your spiritual life. When we finally acknowledge that there is a problem in our relationship with God, we tend to think we need to make huge changes right away. But God responds to little bits of faith, mustard seeds of faith. Jesus taught us that even faith mixed with unbelief is more than sufficient to make it possible for God to do surprising things in our lives.

Taking Further Steps

If you've taken a first step already and have changed a small part of your life, we encourage you to continue on. After putting one principle into practice, try another. A healthy spiritual life grows from the healthy practice of spiritual principles. Once you've made some progress with one tool, we suggest moving on and trying something else. Before too long, you'll have a number of spiritual tools that might help you radically reconstruct your spiritual life.

We also recommend that you find someone you can trust, and share your spiritual practice with that person. Tell that person about the changes you are making, and then keep him or her up-to-date about how you experience those changes. We cannot change on our own. We need God and at least one other person. Whether the other person is a spiritual partner or a friend or a small group with whom we can be real, we need the feedback, wisdom and experience that others can offer.

START HERE

One way to dig deeper into this material would be to invite several others to meet regularly with you to work through this book. The questions at the end of each chapter might be helpful starting points for discussion. If this feels like an appropriate next step for you, we encourage you to spend some extra time thinking and praying your way through "Living in Community" (chap. 10), looking for ways to ensure that the group will be both safe and supportive for all who participate. We also suggest that you read aloud the guidelines for groups listed in that chapter, as a starting point for each group meeting.

Wherever we are in the process of rebuilding our spiritual lives, God is with us. If we are entrenched in the messy and painful demolition stage, God is there with us. If we are exploring new spiritual possibilities and are struggling to trust, God is there with us. And if we have successfully tested the waters of trusting God and are ready to trust even more, God is with us there as well. Every step of the journey, for however long it takes, God's love is with us.

May God grant you the courage, wisdom and serenity you need as you take the next step. May your heart grow daily in its capacity to receive God's love. And may your foundations become securely attached to the bedrock of God's grace.

ADDITIONAL RESOURCES

RECOMMENDED READING

Benner, David. *Surrender to Love: Discovering the Heart of Christian Spirituality.* Downers Grove, Ill.: InterVarsity Press, 2003.

Brother Lawrence. *The Practice of the Presence of God.* New Kensington, Penn.: Whitaker House, 1982.

Foster, Richard J. *Celebration of Discipline: The Path to Spiritual Growth.* New York: HarperOne, 2006.

Johnson, David, and Jeff VanVonderen. *The Subtle Power of Spiritual Abuse: Recognizing and Escaping Spiritual Manipulation and False Spiritual Authority Within the Church.* Minneapolis: Bethany House, 2005.

Kidd, Sue Monk. *When the Heart Waits: Spiritual Direction for Life's Sacred Questions.* San Francisco: HarperSanFrancisco, 1992.

Nouwen, Henri J. M. *The Way of the Heart.* New York: Ballantine, 2003.

Ryan, Dale, and Juanita Ryan. *Rooted in God's Love: Meditations on Biblical Texts for Christians in Recovery.* Brea, Calif.: Christian Recovery International, 2007.

—————. *Spiritual Kindergarten: Christian Perspectives on the Twelve Steps.* Brea, Calif.: Christian Recovery International, 2007.

VanVonderen, Jeff. *Good News for the Chemically Dependent and Those Who Love Them.* Minneapolis: Bethany House, 2004.

RECOMMENDED WEBSITES

Christian Recovery International <www.christianrecovery.com>.

National Association for Christian Recovery (NACR) <www.nacron line.com>.

Recovery University <recoveryu.com>.

Spiritual Abuse Recovery Resources <spiritualabuse.com>.